D0204875

The
Coenzyme
Q10
Phenomenon

The Coenzyme Q10 Phenomenon

STEPHEN T. SINATRA, M.D., F.A.C.C.

Keats Publishing, Inc.　New Canaan, Connecticut

The Coenzyme Q10 Phenomenon is not intended as medical advice. Its intent is solely informational and educational. Please consult a health professional should the need for one be indicated.

THE COENZYME Q10 PHENOMENON
Copyright © 1998 by Stephen T. Sinatra, M.D.
All Rights Reserved

No part of this book may be reproduced in any form without the written consent of the publisher.

Library of Congress Cataloging-in-Publication Data

Sinatra, Stephen T.
    The coenzyme Q10 phenomenon / Stephen T. Sinatra.
        p.   cm.
    Includes bibliographical references and index.
    ISBN 0-87983-957-0
        1. Ubiquinones — Therapeutic use.   2. Ubiquinones —
    Physiological effect.   I. Title.
    RM666.U24S56   1998
    615'.35 — dc21   98-11632
                                                                CIP

Printed in the United States of America

Keats Publishing, Inc.
27 Pine Street (Box 876)
New Canaan, Connecticut 06840-0876
Website Address: www.keats.com

For the late Karl Folkers, the "father of CoQ10," who was one of the greatest chemists of the 20th century. Dr. Folkers, who lived to be more than 90 years old, was a testament to the benefits of Coenzyme Q10. The biomedical and chemical aspects of this miracle nutrient consumed the last 40 years of his life. He never thought of retiring and was actively involved in CoQ10 research right to the end.

In his lifetime, Dr. Folkers won every scientific award short of the Nobel Prize. Unfortunately, he was 20 years ahead of his time and proposed ideas that were not well received by mainstream medicine until recently. Although he was trained by the pharmaceutical industry to develop drugs, Folkers had both the insight and foresight to use biochemical research as the basis for nutritional healing.

Contents

Preface

Hundreds of scientific studies and thousands of clinical applications have documented that Coenzyme Q10, synthesized in every living cell of the human body, may be one of the greatest 20th century medicinal discoveries for the prevention and treatment of disease. The mainstream public is just beginning to understand—and appreciate—the wonders of this nutrient.

Although clinical studies are still in their infancy, this nutrient has already been shown to be a truly powerful healer. It is a nutritional *must* in our quest to stay well and disease-free.

I call CoQ10 *the* miracle nutrient of the fast-approaching 21st century. At the same time, CoQ10 represents a mere fraction of the new tidal wave of metabolic/nutritional healing resources that will increasingly play a major role in integrative medicine.

That's because it has been proven to both *prevent* and *treat* a host of health problems including heart disease, cancer, periodontal disease and neurodegenerative diseases like Alzheimer's. It is also an effective antiaging remedy, offering a better quality of life as we grow older; moreover, it can help overcome male infertility and immune system dysfunction.

Fortunately, this nutrient is available at a time when getting sick in America is fraught with danger, not only to one's health but also to one's pocketbook. Mainstream medicine, caught up in bureaucracy and red tape, can no longer provide us with the kind of personal health care it did when your family doctor made housecalls. Once considered an art, medicine is now big business, controlled by burgeoning conglomerates.

Worse, physicians have lost most, if not all, control over the quality of medicine they now practice. On top of it all, the cost of healthcare is skyrocketing, leaving us all to wonder who's going to pay for it.

Medical Care 2001

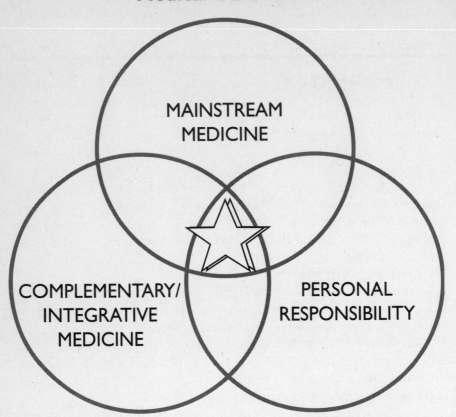

The state of medicine in this country today requires that we take responsibility for our own health and healing. Optimum health embraces a trinity: mainstream medicine, personal responsibility and complementary/integrative methods that really work.

CoQ10 is just one of the many nutrients I use to preserve optimum health; however, it is a vital first step for those with health concerns. This book will provide readers with life-enhancing information as we approach the 21st century.

Acknowledgments

My work and this book would not have been possible without the help and support of the following people who are an important part of my life:

- To Jan DeMarco, R.N., M.S.N. Your endless hours of research, editing, support and love have allowed me to move forward in my mission.
- To my children, March, Step and Drew who all take CoQ10.
- To Peter Langsjoen, M.D., F.A.C.C. and Alena Langsjoen, M.S. for their exceptional work in Coenzyme Q10 research. Your dedication to this healing nutrient will help millions of patients.
- To the late Per Langsjoen who dedicated his life to Coenzyme Q10.
- To Fred Crane, Ph.D., G. P. Littarru, M.D. and Emile Blizakov, M.D., early pioneers in Q10 research who I admire and respect.
- To Jo-Anne Piazza, Stan Jankowitz, Raj Chopra and Mel Rich. Your years of friendship, support and research have allowed us to bring state-of-the-art formulas to many patients who need help.
- To Hemi Bhagavan who helped me with the research on CoQ10.
- To Norman Rothbaum and Phyllis Herman at Keats Publishing.
- To Sun King Wan, M.D., F.A.C.C., Saqib Naseer, M.D., Richard Delany, M.D., F.A.C.C., Harvey Zarren, M.D., F.A.C.C., Lee Cowden, M.D., F.A.C.C., Bruno Cortis, M.D., F.A.C.C., Steven Kunkes, M.D., F.A.C.C., William Frishman, M.D., F.A.C.C., Dan Wise, M.D., F.A.C.C., Steven Horowitz, M.D., F.A.C.C., Fred Vagnini, M.D., F.A.C.C., Jose Seco, M.D., F.A.C.C., and all other cardiological colleagues who believe in the power of Coenzyme Q10.
- To Derrick DeSilva, M.D., Michael Murray, N.D., Julian Whitaker, M.D., Jonathan Wright, M.D. and all other health professionals who use Coenzyme Q10 on a regular basis.

- To Dr. Salvatore Squatrito, Jr. for sharing his clinical data on CoQ10 and periodontal disease.
- To Dr. Steven Novil, Dr. Robert Goldman and Dr. Ronald Klatz at the American Academy for Antiaging Medicine.
- To my colleagues at Phillips Publishing including Bob King, Lorna Newman, Karen Berney, Donna Engelgau, Kate Fiedler and Steve Kupritz.
- To my office staff, especially Donna Chaput and Susan Worona, for their many hours of transcription. Thanks for all your support.
- To Jeannine Cyr-Gluck, the librarian at the Eastern Connecticut Health Network for all the CoQ10 articles you retrieved for me.
- To Anne Sellaro, my publicist. You have more energy than I do!
- To Louise Kay and Tommy Ingram for their courage in sharing their life-and-death struggles with others. To all my other patients who believe in the healing capabilities of Coenzyme Q10.

Introduction

Coenzyme Q10 first came to my attention in 1982 when I read a journal article[1] reporting on its effectiveness in helping patients come off heart-lung bypass, a transition from surgery that is fraught with danger. I was intrigued, so I clipped the article. However, like most of my colleagues at that time in my professional growth and development, I still had some bias against simple nonpharmaceutical compounds, vitamins and cofactors. I failed to appreciate that their effects could be so dramatic.

It took me four years to become convinced enough to let go of my rigid conventional medical thinking. After reading Emile Blizakov's book *The Miracle Nutrient—Coenzyme Q10* in 1986 I began to integrate CoQ10 into my cardiology practice. I was highly impressed with the results and soon became committed to spreading the word about this remarkable compound. In the last dozen years, I have recommended Coenzyme Q10 for thousands of patients in my medical practice and continue to recommend it to the thousands of subscribers who read *HeartSense*, my monthly newsletter.

My passion for CoQ10 today goes well beyond its use in clinical cardiology. CoQ10 is an important medicinal that can alleviate a much wider range of human suffering. Educating my medical colleagues and the general public about CoQ10 has become a mission for me. I have published papers on it in both the medical and lay literature and, with the assistance of pharmacists, chemists and other doctors, I have participated in double-blind research regarding the technological and scientific aspects of how CoQ10 is best absorbed by the body.

The body requires certain blood levels of CoQ10 to function properly, and when blood levels fall an increased vulnerability to disease and premature aging occurs. It is my belief that supplemental CoQ10 not only improves the quality of life in patients with diseases, but also saves lives.

The purpose of this book is to increase public awareness of the profound clinical implications of this vital compound. It is my hope that this communication will deliver the CoQ10 story to as many people as possible.

To lecture and report on CoQ10, both nationally and internationally, to various audiences including physicians, scientists, media and lay people, continues to give me great pleasure.

In her recent best-selling book *Miracle Cures*,[2] Jean Carper lists Coenzyme Q10 as miracle cure #1. She states "it is the heart medicine used around the world, and if your doctor doesn't know about it, you can easily get it on your own; it could save your life." In this one sentence, Carper has captured the essence of CoQ10. Read on for more evidence about the miracle healing properties of CoQ10.

PART I

Fundamentals of Coenzyme Q10

CoQ10: A Miracle in Our Midst

In October 1996 I had just returned from a conference in Florida when I got a call from a man who asked me to take his mother as a patient in transfer from another hospital. She was 79 years old and had been admitted to a community hospital in Connecticut with heart failure complicated by pneumonia. It was the first time she had ever been in the hospital in her entire life, except for childbirth. Previously, she was a healthy, vibrant woman.

She had been on a ventilator for three-and-a-half weeks, receiving powerful steroids and high concentrations of oxygen. Her days were numbered. Her son, a Ph.D. biochemist, was an expert in CoQ10 and other nutritional supplements. He asked the doctors at the community hospital if he could place his mother on CoQ10, but they refused. He then proceeded to bring in reams of research literature, but the doctors still wouldn't hear of it. He was very upset. He even went to the hospital administrators—they asked him to leave the hospital. Lawyers became involved. It was a disaster.

Because of their lack of knowledge and their fear and bias against nonconventional supplementation and because CoQ10 was not on formulary in the hospital, the doctors refused to consider this alternative treatment for the woman, and her concerned family was labeled "interfering." The physicians asked the family to end life support, but twice the daughter refused to "pull the plug."

When the son called me on the telephone, I was very direct. "I can't take your mother in transfer. They will have to bag-breathe her for over 40 minutes in an ambulance. She'll probably die." He was quick to reply. "At least with you she will have a fighting chance because, if she stays where she is, she's certainly going to die." I told him that if his mother was transferred in the ambulance, I could not be responsible. He was willing to take the chance, and she was transferred.

When I first saw Mary in the intensive care unit at Manchester Memorial Hospital, she was semicomatose, respirator-dependent, and responded only to verbal command and pain stimulation. Her pulmonary care was similar to that received at the previous hospital. The only change in her therapy was nutritional: 450 mg of Coenzyme Q10 was given through her feeding tube daily. Mary also received a multivitamin/mineral preparation that I had developed as well as one gram of magnesium intravenously on a daily basis. Although I had some hope for Mary, the other critical care doctors and nurses were extremely skeptical of using CoQ10 in this life-threatening case despite the fact that CoQ10 had been on formulary at our hospital for several years. What we were all about to observe was truly a resurrection.

On the third day, Mary started to come out of her coma. After ten days, she was weaned off the ventilator. Four days later, sitting up in a wheelchair and using only supplemental oxygen, she was discharged to an extended care facility.

I have had the good fortune to see Mary in my office on several occasions since that time. She is enjoying a good quality of life on conventional medical therapy plus 360 mg of CoQ10 per day. When I last spoke with her family, she was reorganizing a vast library of about 3,000 books.

For me, Mary's story is not unusual. I have personally treated and heard of many anecdotal cases of people seemingly "left for dead" who have been similarly resurrected by the compound called Coenzyme Q10, which I believe is a proven miracle nutrient.

It is unthinkable for me to practice good cardiology without the help of Coenzyme Q10. And, for the thousands of people with cardiac conditions so severe that they need a heart transplant, CoQ10 may be a suitable alternative that not only enhances quality of life but extends survival as well. For some, it serves as a potent medicinal while for others it may literally buy time until a donor heart is available.

Research has shown that CoQ10 is an indisputable heart remedy, but most doctors have never even heard of it. And even those physicians who are aware of CoQ10 most likely dismiss it. Why is this so?

Although Coenzyme Q10 represents the greatest potential break-through for cardiovascular disease and some other illnesses as well, the resistance of the medical profession to using this essential nutrient represents one of the greatest potential tragedies in medicine.

As a cardiologist myself, I believe that Coenzyme Q10 is one of the greatest medicinal advances in the 20th century for the treatment of heart disease.

Twenty-seven thousand citations on the Internet alone cite that CoQ10 has proven benefits for treating a wide variety of degenerative diseases, especially clinical cardiac conditions including congestive heart failure, high blood pressure, angina ("heart cramp") and ar-rhythmia as well as other cardiological situations.

Yet, despite a large body of available information, a therapeutic de-scription in a 1997 textbook of mainstream cardiology[1] and the fact that CoQ10 is used by many board-certified cardiologists in this coun-try as well as in western Europe and Japan, the nutrient is still virtu-ally ignored by the majority of clinical cardiologists and most of the conventional medical establishment as well.

Unfortunately, the many patients who are not helped by conven-tional treatments alone, but could be supported by the addition of Coenzyme Q10, will never even be given a chance to receive it. This was certainly true for my patient, Mary, before she was transferred to Manchester Memorial Hospital.

It is also tragic that, in addition to the widespread ignorance about nutritional medicine, there is also such negative bias against it. The re-jection of Coenzyme Q10 as a potent, nonpharmacological treatment defies the imagination. It is apparently difficult for highly trained med-ical personnel, well-versed in pharmacology and technology, to believe that anything so simple and so natural can be as effective as the highly engineered drugs modern medicine has to offer. Most American cardi-ologists cannot acknowledge that a natural substance not manufac-tured by pharmaceutical industry giants could be so valuable. All of these factors have rendered Coenzyme Q10 a victim of politics, bias, insufficient marketing, economics and ignorance of the results of real science.

Another blockade has been the patent issue. Since Coenzyme Q10 is not patentable, there is no economic incentive for major pharmacological companies to develop it as a product. Although pharmaceutical companies will usually encourage their sales representatives to start a campaign to educate physicians about new products, the distributors of Coenzyme Q10 do not have the financial and physical resources to "detail" CoQ10 as a major medicinal. Such an effort is just too costly for any company to take on when it cannot expect to have the exclusive patent or corner on the market.

Today, anyone can purchase any number of brands of Coenzyme Q10 in a health food store. Unfortunately, without massive physician education supported by ongoing research and pharmaceutical representation, Coenzyme Q10 will probably remain controversial until the evidence on the importance of this nutrient becomes so compelling that it will finally receive the respect it deserves.

I am very concerned about the misrepresentation of Q10 and continue to advocate this vitamin/nutrient to the public and my peers. Two years ago, I wrote the following response to a biased article on CoQ10 in a well-respected medical newsletter.

As a subscriber to the *Harvard Heart Letter* for the past several years, I was greatly disappointed to read your February 1996 article on Coenzyme Q10. I thought one of your missions was to present accurate medical information. I felt your article on Coenzyme Q10 was full of negative bias and attitude. As an author and lecturer on nutritional healing as well as a user of Coenzyme Q10 for, perhaps, the last decade, I have read hundreds of articles in the medical literature with studies and numbers far exceeding what your article indicates. In addition, the last sentence of the article reveals that results are not likely to be dramatic. I can tell you from my clinical experience that I have even seen patients refuse cardiac transplantation because of their tremendous improvement in quality of life on Coenzyme Q10. CoQ10 is a very valuable adjunct for many patients when used in combination with conventional cardiology in the treatment of congestive heart failure.

The article also reported that "none of the physicians consulted in the preparation of this article recommended the use of Coenzyme Q10." This is absolutely outrageous. Were physicians from Japan or Western Europe consulted? Or what about physicians who use Coenzyme Q10 on a day-to-day basis such as myself or many other highly trained, board-certified cardiologists?

Also, were you aware that Coenzyme Q10 is on formulary in Japanese hospitals? Although Coenzyme Q10 is perhaps not the next "aspirin," as you suggest, in many people it has made a big difference in the quality of their lives.

When I see an article like this, I question the validity of your publication. For this reason, I must cancel my subscription.

Sincerely,

Stephen T. Sinatra, M.D., F.A.C.C. March 18, 1996.

Am I too passionate about CoQ10? Maybe so. But when you hear the entire story of this nutrient, I think you will share my enthusiasm. It is my belief that in the very near future the evidence on the importance of this nutrient will become so compelling that finally Coenzyme Q10 will receive the respect it deserves. I see the bias of the medical community against Q10 as very similar to its 25-year-long rejection of the homocysteine theory of Kilmer McCully, the brilliant pioneer in homocysteine research.

Clinical research has demonstrated that serious Coenzyme Q10 deficiencies exist in our population due to a multitude of factors, including the fact that CoQ10 production gradually declines in the body with aging. CoQ10 supplementation has been shown to increase blood levels of this essential nutrient resulting in many clinical benefits.

The recovery of an ailing heart, such as in the case of Mary, is but a fraction of the entire CoQ10 story. This amazing nutrient is being used for a wide variety of serious degenerative diseases, including heart disease, high blood pressure, cancer, periodontal disease, diabetes, neurological disorders and even aging itself. In addition, Coenzyme Q10 is considered a medicinal for relieving male infertility and has the ability to support the immune system in the HIV/AIDS syndrome. In fact, CoQ10 seems to support almost any tissue in need of assistance, repair or help.

But before we discuss the clinical applications of CoQ10, let's start with the discovery and 40-year history of Q10 research to set the groundwork.

2

History of CoQ10

Like many other incredible breakthroughs in metabolic medicine, the discovery of Coenzyme Q10 was actually the result of search for a vitamin that could fill a gap in the mitochondrial energy conversion process. Researchers were performing experiments on beef heart mitochondria at the University of Wisconsin Laboratory in 1957 under the direction of Dr. D. Green when Dr. Fred L. Crane[1] noticed yellow crystals in a test tube containing lipid extracted from mitochondria. One day, out of curiosity, Dr. Crane dissolved the yellow crystalline substance and measured its light absorptive spectrum. From the spectrum it was identified as a quinone. He sent a few milligrams to Dr. Karl Folkers, who reisolated it at the Merck, Sharpe and Dohme Laboratories in Rahway, N.J. Folkers determined its chemical structure to be 2,3 dimethoxy-5 methyl-6-decaprenyl-1, 4-benzoquinone.

In 1957, Dr. D.E. Wolf and his colleagues at the Merck Pharmaceutical Company reported on the chemical structure of this quinone. Q defines its membership in the quinone group, and the figure 10 identifies the number of isoprenoid units in its side chain. Dr. R.A. Morton[2] called the Q10 compound *ubiquinone* because of its widespread appearance in living organisms.

Dr. Folkers, leader of the Merck research group, became so intrigued that he proceeded to spearhead pioneer studies into the biochemistry, action and clinical aspects of this new discovery, now called Coenzyme Q10. Merck, although sitting on the potential to investigate and develop Coenzyme Q10, dropped the ball at this point; thus it was the Japanese, in 1963, who began testing the supplement on humans on an individual case basis.

The History of CoQ10

1957   CoQ10 first isolated from beef heart by
            Frederick Crane.

1958   Karl Folkers at Merck, Sharpe & Dohme deter-
            mines the precise chemical structure.

1961   CoQ10 identified in non-mitochondrial mem-
            branes by T. Ramasarma and coworkers.

Mid-1960s   Professor Yamamura of Japan is the first to use
            Coenzyme Q7 (related compound) in congestive
            heart failure.

1972   Dr. Littarru (Italy) and Dr. Folkers (U.S.) document
            a CoQ10 deficiency in human heart disease.

Mid-1970s   Japanese perfect industrial technology of fermenta-
            tion to produce pure CoQ10 in significant quanti-
            ties.

Karl Folkers, M.D., the author and Raj Chopra at the Academy of Antiaging Medicine Conference, December 1996.

1976   CoQ10 is placed on formulary in Japanese hospitals.

1978   Peter Mitchell receives Nobel Prize for CoQ10 and energy transfer.

1980s   Enthusiasm for CoQ10 leads to tremendous increase in number and size of clinical studies around the world.

1985   Dr. Per Langsjoen in Texas reports the profound impact CoQ10 has in cardiomyopathy in double-blind studies.

1990s   Explosion of use of CoQ10 in health food industry.

1992   CoQ10 placed on formulary at Manchester Memorial Hospital, Manchester, Connecticut.

1996   9th international conference on CoQ10 in Ancona, Italy. Scientists and physicians report on a variety of medical conditions improved by CoQ10 administration. Blood levels of at least 2.5 ug/ml and preferably higher required for most medicinal purposes.

1996–97   Gel-Tec, a division of Tishcon Corp., under the leadership of Raj Chopra, develops the "Biosolv process," allowing for greater bioavailability of supplemental CoQ10 in the body.

1997   CoQ10 included in textbooks of mainstream cardiology.

The first organized clinical trial of Coenzyme Q10 in human subjects was performed by Dr. Y. Yamamura and his colleagues at Osaka University in 1965, where the nutrient was given to patients with heart disease. In 1971, Drs. Folkers (USA) and Littarru (Italy) reported that patients with periodontal disease were often deficient in Coenzyme Q10, and one year later they demonstrated a deficiency of CoQ10 in cases of human heart disease.[3]

In 1973, Dr. Folkers completed a double-blind study with Dr. Matsumura (Japan), employing CoQ10 for gum disease, and reported it as superior to the current treatment for periodontal diseases. Not long afterward, Dr. E.G. Wilkinson, prominent U.S. Air Force periodontal specialist, confirmed that not only did he too find CoQ10 deficiencies in patients with gum disease, but that oral doses of the supplement promoted healing.

It was not until 1974 that large enough quantities of CoQ10 could be harvested to support organized clinical trials in large groups of people. Scientists in Japan perfected the industrial technology to produce pure CoQ10 in sufficient quantities for distribution. So it was at this crossroads that CoQ10 gained widespread acceptance in Japan and became more available for those with heart disease.

Meanwhile, one night at about 3:00 A.M., English scientist Peter Mitchell was struggling to sleep. Looking at an incomplete schema in his mind's eye, he suddenly had an "Aha!" experience and realized the solution to a complicated puzzle he had been trying to piece together. Subsequently, in 1978, he was given the Nobel Prize for hypothesizing how CoQ10 works and describing energy transfer processes within the mitochondria of the cell.[4] The momentum continued to build in the latter half of the 1970s.

By 1982, CoQ10 had reached a level of consumption in Japan that rivaled that country's top five medications. It has been Japanese, and later European scientists and physicians, who have conducted the majority of clinical trials employing CoQ10. In a 1985 review article, Dr. Yamamura[5] listed 67 clinical studies that evaluated CoQ10 in cases of heart muscle disease, arrhythmias and heart damage from drugs, high blood pressure and stroke. At the same time, Per Langsjoen, M.D. in Texas, testing CoQ10 in double-blind fashion, reported on CoQ10 as a valuable nutrient for cardiomyopathy.[6]

Just one year later (1986), the prestigious Priestley Medal of the American Chemical Society was awarded to Dr. Folkers, often called the "father of CoQ10," for his research into this nutrient as well as others. At about the same time, Lars Ernster of Sweden expanded on Coenzyme Q10's significance as a free radical scavenger.[7]

In the 1990s, Coenzyme Q10 became a top-selling supplement in health food stores, where consumers, reading about its healing potential for so many medical problems, began buying it for themselves. Today, the Internet is crowded with CoQ10 wholesalers and those who just want a billboard on which to place their latest CoQ10 success story.

As of 1997 there have been over 100 observational, epidemiological and population studies on Coenzyme Q10, and currently there are at least 19 placebo-controlled trials, 16 showing benefits and 3 reporting no significant therapeutic responses. Two of the studies that showed no benefit were conducted by the same group of authors who failed to include research design blood levels of CoQ10 before and after treatment. Even the authors of these negative studies admit that plasma levels should be measured to demonstrate sufficient absorption of CoQ10.

From 1976 through 1998 there have been ten international symposia on the biochemical and clinical aspects of Coenzyme Q10. These symposia alone have compiled over 350 papers, presented by over 200 different physicians and scientists from 18 different countries, who have investigated Coenzyme Q10 supplementation in a wide range of medical disorders.[8–35]

But, in spite of all this published research, very few American physicians have heard of CoQ10, know how it works or recommend it to those patients whom it would benefit. Those who could guide the public best about when and how to use CoQ10 are disinterested in it.

So what is it that has caused American doctors to ignore the potential of this life-essential nutrient? The research scientists are the only ones in this country who seem to understand the incredible healing capacity of Q10, and they struggle to get the word out to physicians. As a physician who uses Q10 on a daily basis and who has listened to the basic research, my mission now is to tell you the truth about this amazing nutrient. But first, let me now explain what Q10 is and how it works in our bodies.

3

Definition and Biochemistry of CoQ10

Coenzyme Q10, or ubiquinone, is a naturally occurring substance that is found in virtually all cells of the human body. Naturally found in foods as well, the usual average daily dietary intake is approximately ten milligrams per day. However, the amount received from dietary sources is insufficient to produce any substantial clinical effects, especially in those with pathological situations such as periodontal disease, high blood pressure, heart disease, impaired immunity and so on. Although some Coenzyme Q10 is present in most plant and animal cells, it is found in larger concentrations in beef heart, pork, sardines, anchovies, mackerel, salmon, broccoli, spinach and nuts. Coenzyme Q10 is also synthesized in all tissues of the body.

The biosynthesis of CoQ10, which is the dominant source in man, involves a complex process requiring the amino acid tyrosine and at least eight vitamins and several trace elements. The quinone ring of Coenzyme Q10 is synthesized from tyrosine. The polyisoprenoid side-chain is formed from acetyl CoA. Thus, the structure of Coenzyme Q10 includes a benzoquinone or chemical compound containing a six-carbon benzene ring. The isoprenoid side chain is attached at the sixth carbon on the ring.[1] The number of isoprene units varies from zero to ten, depending upon the animal species. In humans, Coenzyme Q10 has ten isoprene units—thus the name Coenzyme Q10.

A deficiency in any of the required amino acids, vitamins and other minerals impairs the endogenous formation of CoQ10 in the body. Without CoQ10, the body cannot survive. As CoQ10 levels in the cells

Biochemical Structure of Coenzyme Q10

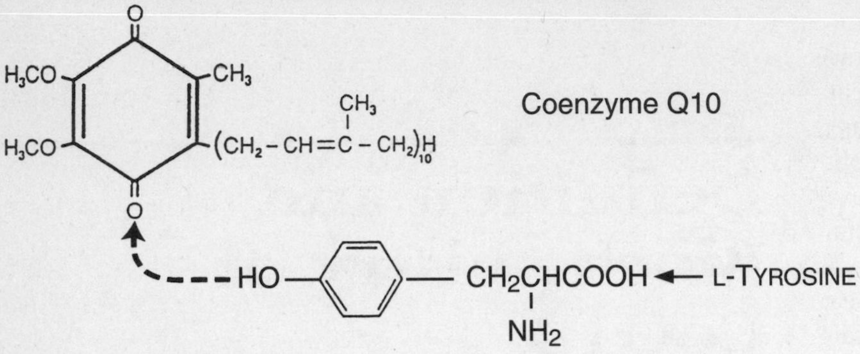

Figure 1

fall, so does general health. What is CoQ10, and why is it so important and crucial for survival?

CoQ10, as a fat-soluble compound, functions as a coenzyme in the energy-producing metabolic pathways of every cell of the body. It has a unique capacity to transfer an ionic charge across membranes. The ionic charge drives the production of ATP which is necessary for muscle contraction and other vital functions of the body. It also has a powerful antioxidant activity.

As an antioxidant, the reduced form of Coenzyme Q10 inhibits lipid peroxidation (oxidation of fats) in both cell membranes and serum low-density lipoproteins (LDL) and also protects proteins and mitochondrial DNA from oxidative damage. Coenzyme Q10 also plays a vital role in combating free radical stress.[2] Let me explain what this means.

FREE RADICALS AND DISEASE

While we cannot see the effects of oxidation (free radical damage) in our body, we are all familiar with common examples of oxidation in the world around us, like the browning of a freshly cut apple or the rusting of metal. Unlike molecular oxygen, oxygen-free radicals are highly reactive and can cause damage to cellular components if not controlled properly. Oxidation results from the breakdown of oxygen molecules as they combine with other molecules in our body. Such free radicals are the result of the body's normal metabolism of the foods we eat, or it can be produced in the body as a result of external forces such as radiation, air pollution, alcohol or heavy metal intoxication; use of pharmaceutical and over-the-counter drugs, infections; or damage can even occur due to strenuous exercise. Under any of these circumstances, excessive free radical production results.

Free radicals are highly reactive molecules produced during various reactions in the body. Interfering with enzymatic activities, free radicals do their damage by attacking cells in the body. Because these bombarding molecules have unpaired electrons, they collide like unguided missiles, causing disruptions of cells, membranes and even DNA itself. The body struggles to defend itself, engaging in a continuous biochemical battle to neutralize the free radicals resulting from invading toxins (rancid fats, heavy metals, cigarette smoke, etc.) and the over-stressed immune system.

During this molecular warfare, the toxic waste of combat begins to accumulate in the body, producing an enormous metabolic stress which, over time, can lead to disease.

During free radical stress, the oxidants act like invaders, taking away electrons from precious molecules. The antioxidants that we naturally produce in the body or which we add to our diet, such as in foods or supplements rich in vitamins C, E and the minerals selenium and zinc, help to cancel out the chemical activity of free radicals and protect our cells. Like suicide pilots who sacrifice themselves for the benefit of their cause, antioxidants surrender electrons easily in these metabolic reactions and function to neutralize the invading oxidants.

Since the antioxidant activity of CoQ10 is directly related to energy-carrier function, CoQ10 molecules can generally undergo oxidation/reduction. As CoQ10 accepts electrons it becomes reduced, and as it gives up electrons it becomes oxidized. In the reduced form, Coenzyme Q10 can give up electrons quickly and easily and thus act as a powerful antioxidant against free radicals.[3] Since free radicals contain highly reactive molecules with unpaired electrons, CoQ10's remarkable donor activity makes it an ideal antioxidant. Acting like a bodyguard, Q10's actions protect the body.

Coenzyme Q10, like other antioxidants, can engulf free radicals before they do their damage, protecting DNA, cellular membranes and even various enzyme systems involved in the metabolism of food and oxygen in the body. We know that the health of every cell in the body depends upon the balance of free radicals and antioxidants. It has been theorized that such antioxidant activity has been needed for millions of years, ever since oxygen appeared in the earth's atmosphere.

Although oxygen is necessary for aerobic life, the breakdown (metabolism) of oxygen has metabolic consequences. Free radicals, the oxidant byproducts of normal metabolism, are causative agents of the degenerative diseases of the 20th century, such as cancer and heart disease, and also culprits in aging itself.

But not all free radicals are bad. Free radicals also play a key role in normal biological functions that support necessary life processes such as mitochondrial respiration,[4] platelet activation[5] and prostaglandin synthesis.[6] Thus, free radicals have a dark side and a bright side. This paradox of free radical chemistry has generated tremendous interest in the healthcare profession, especially for those interested in aging and preventive medicine.

Since the electron-rich reduced forms of Coenzyme Q10, vitamin E and other antioxidants, support antioxidant defenses, their presence becomes vital in strategies to prevent free radical damage and premature aging. The antioxidant activity of CoQ10 is especially noteworthy in other areas as well. Because the oxidized form of vitamin E can be reduced by Coenzyme Q10, vitamin E regeneration is enhanced. As a recycler of vitamin E, CoQ10 makes its antioxidant partner more available to help trap free radicals before they do their damage.

Scientific research has demonstrated that a combination supplementation of vitamin E and CoQ10 makes LDL more resistant to oxidation than when vitamin E is used alone.[7,8] Because the oxidation of LDL is the pivotal step in the cause of atherosclerosis, this finding has major implications in the prevention of coronary heart disease.

It is also important to note the membrane-stabilizing activity of CoQ10 and its very recently discovered favorable effects on platelets[9] and platelet function. All of these properties of CoQ10 enhance its antiaging benefits.

ENERGY AND ATP

CoQ10's bioenergetic activity is probably its most important function. The term "bioenergetic" is used in the field of biochemistry to describe compounds that support cellular energy. Such energy enhancement occurs in the mitochondria (the powerful furnaces that generate energy in cells). It is there, in the so-called cellular boiler room, that Coenzyme Q10 acts as an essential component in the electron transport chain where metabolic energy is released. It is the generation of this chemical energy that supplies the vital force so necessary for life.

The healthy operation of the human energy system requires the adequate formation of energy. This process is dependent upon a sufficient intake of oxygen and essential nutrients, vitamins and cofactors. The end product is the pulsation of healthy cells. Every living cell has pulsatory activity. The cells have resting as well as generative phases. The maintenance of proper cellular functioning depends upon a multitude of complex variables.

A deficiency or an imbalance in any part of the system may contribute, over time, to the impaired functioning of cells, tissues, organs and eventually the entire body. We need to view the concept of energy as both quantitative and qualitative. A proper balance of oxygen and nutritional components, such as vitamins, minerals, enzymes and cofactors, is required on a second-to-second basis for the cells to function optimally. It is this total concept of energy that demonstrates that Coenzyme Q10 is an essential component to maintain the energetic vital life force.

CoQ10 is involved in the reactions of at least three mitochondrial enzymes, rendering it the essential component of the electron transport chain. In a series of complex reactions involving pathways in the mitochondrial chain, the synthesis of adenosine triphosphate (ATP) occurs.[10]

ATP is a high-energy phosphate compound necessary to fuel all cellular functions. Think of ATP as a "high-octane fuel" used for all the energetic transactions in the body. We may think that we eat only to satisfy hunger or our taste buds or to socialize. But the truth is we consume food to get the energy sources required to generate ATP, the body's major form of stored energy that ultimately drives the machinery of our bodies.

All cellular function depends on an adequate supply of ATP. ATP facilitates the chemical energy released by oxidation and other cellular reactions, maintaining the essential and the diverse functions of life. CoQ10's role as a mobile electron carrier in the mitochondrial electron transfer chain makes it the pivotal nutrient for the production of cellular energy. In biochemical terms, Coenzyme Q10 supports every cell in the human body by generating an electrical charge on the mitochondrial membrane which can drive ATP production. It is this key bioenergetic property that makes Coenzyme Q10 so unique. In simple language, Coenzyme Q10 provides the spark in the mitochondria of each cell to initiate the energy process. This is why CoQ10 is vital for life itself.

Think of the body as a fine-tuned car. Functioning on low levels of Coenzyme Q10 would be similar to running a car on a low-octane fuel. With such poor octane energy fuel, the cylinders in the car's high-performance engine (where the gasoline is ignited) would not have sufficient force to move the pistons evenly. The energy that then drives the car would be inadequate, resulting in misfiring pistons and sluggish, undependable movement. Similarly, the human body must have high-octane fuel to create the energy to carry on the basic processes of life, such as respiration and the breakdown and assimilation of foods. And for more complex operations, such as the pulsation of the heart, walking, mental activity, playing golf and so forth, there is an even higher demand for energy. But where does this energy come from?

A major part of energy production in the body is the result of this complicated biochemical process, starting with the oxidative phosphorylation pathways in which ATP is formed (see figure 2). So without Coenzyme Q10, there would be no "spark" in the mitochondria to ignite this energy transfer. Without energy-rich compounds of ATP, the body would stall and cease to function.

In essence, without adequate energy the cells would be inefficient, lackluster, and vulnerable to free radical attack and disease. When a deficiency of Coenzyme Q10 exists, the cellular "engines" misfire and, over time, they may eventually fail or even die. The bioenergetics of a failing heart or a failing immune system will inevitably lead to the weakening of all the natural defenses against disease and premature aging.

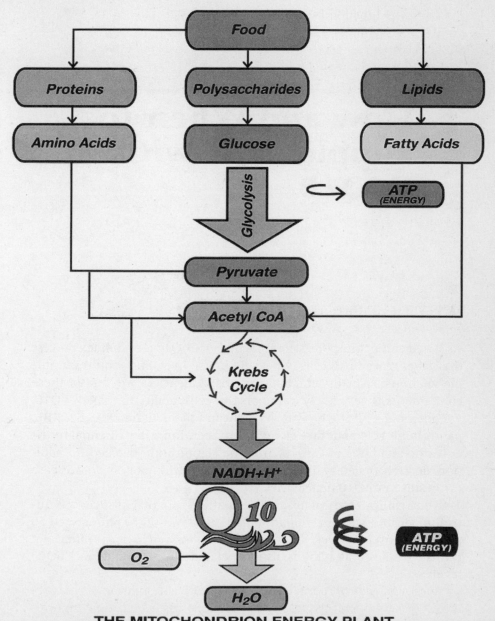

THE MITOCHONDRION ENERGY PLANT
Adapted from ENERGY AND DEFENSE by Prof. GIAN PAOLO LITTARRU
Publ. Casa Editrice Scientifica Internazionale, Rome, Italy, 1995

Figure 2

4

How and When to Supplement with CoQ10

WHY DO DEFICIENCIES OCCUR?

As stated earlier, the body's manufacture of CoQ10 is a complex process that takes place in all cells, especially in the liver, and requires multiple vitamins, cofactors and amino acids. A deficiency in any of these components is very likely to impair the cells' ability to make CoQ10.

For example, if the body is deficient in folate, vitamins C, B12, B6, pantothenic acid and trace elements, to mention a few essential nutrients, the synthesis of CoQ10 could be significantly blocked. In addition, decreased dietary intake, chronic malnutrition or chronic disease can result in CoQ10 deficiencies.

In one clinical study of hospitalized patients on total intravenous nutrition without vitamin support, blood levels of CoQ10 plummeted 50 percent in just one week.[1] It has also been observed in both animal and human studies that aging is also associated with a decline in CoQ10 levels.[2]

Moreover, environmental stressors as well as lifestyle factors may reduce CoQ10 in body tissues. One lifestyle stressor is chronic high-intensity exercise. When athletes have been studied, low blood levels of CoQ10 have been observed, most probably because of the increased metabolic demands of chronically exercising muscles, resulting in an excess of free radicals.[3]

Other environmental factors that may result in CoQ10 deficiencies include cholesterol-lowering drugs such as the HMG-CoA reductase inhibitors.[4] Statin-like drugs, such as Lovastatin, Simvastatin, Pravastatin, to mention a few, often used to treat patients with high cholesterol levels, are in this category of pharmaceuticals.

The population being treated with these HMG-CoA reductase inhibitors to lower serum cholesterol is also at risk for CoQ10 depletion. Cholesterol production, as well as endogenous pathways for CoQ10 production, are both compromised by these drugs.

BIOSYNTHETIC PATHWAY OF CHOLESTEROL

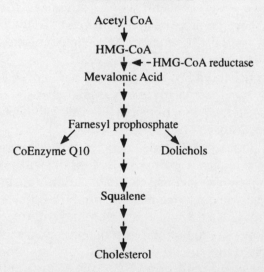

Acetyl CoA

HMG-CoA ← - HMG-CoA reductase

Mevalonic Acid

Farnesyl prophosphate

CoEnzyme Q10   Dolichols

Squalene

Cholesterol

The enzyme 3-hydroxy-3-methylglutaryl Coenzyme A (HMG-CoA) reductase is necessary for the conversion of HMG-CoA to mevalonic acid, an early step in biosynthesis of cholesterol. Because mevalonic acid is also a precursor of Coenzyme Q10 via a branch of the cholesterol biosynthetic pathway. HMG-CoA reductase inhibitors could reduce serum concentrations of Coenzyme Q10.

It is extremely important that physicians be aware of the potential for statins to adversely affect CoQ10 levels. This effect certainly has major implications and ramifications for patients with cardiac disease. It is especially crucial that patients with congestive heart failure or an overactive thyroid be given additional supplemental doses of CoQ10 to offset the depleting effects of these cholesterol-reducing agents.

Moreover, when considering the free radical oxidation mechanism in arteriosclerosis, a decline in CoQ10 reserves may also adversely affect the course of arteriosclerosis *despite* optimal reduction of LDL cholesterol. Certainly, the adverse metabolic effect of these drugs requires further investigation.[5]

Perhaps the greatest source of CoQ10 deficiencies appears in tissues that are metabolically active, such as those found in the heart,[6,7] immune system, gingiva and an overactive thyroid gland.[8]

An overactive thyroid or even a pulsating heart, for that matter, requires additional Coenzyme Q10 support. Although Coenzyme Q10 is found in relatively high concentrations in the liver, the kidneys and the lungs, the heart requires the highest levels of ATP activity[9] because it is continually aerobic. Coenzyme Q10 support is essential for the healthy heart and critical for the failing one.

Tissue deficiencies and low serum blood levels of CoQ10 have been reported across a wide range of cardiovascular diseases, including congestive heart failure,[6,7] hypertension,[10] aortic valvular disease[11] and coronary artery disease.[12]

In summary, Coenzyme Q10 deficiencies may occur as a result of insufficient dietary intake, impairment in CoQ10 synthesis, drug interactions, environmental factors, excessive utilization by tissues or a combination of any of these factors. The profound effects of CoQ10 deficiency have stimulated clinical research into the role of exogenous supplementation as an appropriate therapeutic intervention.

Animal studies have shown that CoQ10 supplementation increases both tissue levels and mitochondrial levels of CoQ10.[13] Human experimental and clinical data have also provided extensive evidence that CoQ10 supplementation can increase blood levels in those with severe heart disease. So we know that it is possible to correct CoQ10 deficiencies by oral supplementation.

However, it is important to look at issues of therapeutic bioavailability and absorption of CoQ10 whenever we consider employing this nutrient. The case of a patient with refractory heart failure follows. For this woman, the right CoQ10 dose made all the difference. Ultimately she was successfully managed as a result of an "error" in dosage that for her made the difference between life and death.

A CASE OF SEVERE CONGESTIVE HEART FAILURE

When she was 60 years of age, L.G. first developed symptoms of congestive heart failure (CHF), a condition in which the heart becomes congested with blood and is dangerously weakened.

L.G.'s heart failure began with a long-standing high blood pressure which had weakened her left ventricle. By age 67 she was congested by the fluid in her lungs (pulmonary edema), and her ejection fraction (EF—the percentage of blood pumped from the left ventricle with each heartbeat) was reduced to 35 percent. The normal range is 50–70 percent. After a second episode of pulmonary edema, L.G. agreed to cardiac catheterization (angiogram), which showed an enlarged, stretched and weakened left ventricle and normal coronary arteries. She was treated with the usual pharmacological drugs for CHF.

Although L.G.'s quality of life was generally satisfactory, she suffered from intermittent bouts of CHF, and her health progressively went downhill. By the time I met her, L.G. was almost 80 years old and struggling for every breath.

In October 1994, L.G. weighed only 77 pounds and was suffering from severe weakness and weight loss (end-stage cardiac cachexia). The echocardiogram showed a "leaky valve" and an EF of only 15 percent, barely enough to support a bed-to-chair lifestyle. I decided to prescribe 30 mg of CoQ10 three times a day (90 mg/day), my comfortable dosing level at that time. Despite the addition of this alternative therapy, L.G. developed marked edema, ascites (a collection of fluids in body cavities, especially the abdomen) and severe fatigue. Her breathing became so labored that she required two lung taps to withdraw the excess fluid from her chest. L.G. remained homebound. She was slowly dying.

I shared L.G.'s great disappointment in the face of her terminal situation, but then a miracle happened. L.G. accidentally started taking 300 mg of CoQ10 daily—more than triple the dose she had become accustomed to taking! Her son had mistakenly purchased 100 mg capsules instead of the usual 30 mg supplements. Four weeks later, L.G. experienced a steady and marked improvement, so I continued her on the 300 mg dose.

Three months later she became more active and mobile. A repeat echocardiogram proved that her ejection fraction had risen from about

15 percent to 20 percent (a $^{1}/_{3}$ increase). In addition, the ultrasound of her heart demonstrated a reduction in her valve leakage.

A full year after she began taking CoQ10 supplements, and eight months after I maintained her on a dosage of 300 mg daily, L.G. was shopping and visiting relatives. She became so active, in fact, that she fell down and fractured her hip! Previously considered a high surgical risk, L.G. underwent a successful hip replacement operation. On 300 mg of Twin Lab's CoQ10 daily, her blood level was 4.8 ug/ml, an ideal blood level for her severe cardiac condition. Unfortunately, L.G.'s battle with CHF ended in January 1998. However, the fact that she enjoyed a good quality of life for three years while on high dose CoQ10 is a testament to the healing power of this nutrient in extremely ill people.

SUPPLEMENTATION WITH COQ10

What can we learn from L.G.'s case? First of all, research indicates that if levels of CoQ10 decline by 25 percent, our organs may become deficient and impaired. When levels decline by 75 percent, serious tissue damage and even death may occur.[14,15] It has also been determined by advanced blood level technology that heart tissue levels of CoQ10 are lower in cases of advanced congestive heart failure. Since myocardial tissue levels of CoQ10 may be restored significantly by oral supplementation, the use of Coenzyme Q10 therapy should be the first defense against congestive heart failure. How much CoQ10 is needed?

Although the cardiovascular literature is filled with multiple studies showing the positive effects of CoQ10 supplements for cardiac patients, the usual recommended dosage is still only 90 mg to 150 mg daily. But, as the case of L.G. clearly teaches us, many patients simply do not respond to such minimal doses. When I have critically ill patients like L.G., I ask myself three questions when considering the CoQ10 dose:

1. Is the dose sufficient to raise the patient's blood level of CoQ10?
2. Does the CoQ10 preparation the patient is taking actually deliver the amount of CoQ10 that is stated on the bottle?
3. How do I know the patient's level of CoQ10 without drawing blood levels?

An adequate dose of CoQ10 will usually result in symptom improvement. If there is a lack of response to a low dose of CoQ10, a higher dose may be indicated. Certainly this was the case for L.G., who required high supplemental doses of CoQ10 to attain a significant blood level with a therapeutic effect.

I have learned one key thing from many patients like L.G.: if the initial response to low doses of CoQ10 is poor, we need not give up. Instead we need to be more aggressive, increase the dosage and maintain it over time. With this aggressive approach, more patients can recapture their quality of life. It is the sickest patients, with the most compromised quality of life, who stand to gain the most from high doses of CoQ10.

This brings me to the second lesson I have recently learned: not all CoQ10 preparations are the same because some CoQ10 preparations are less bioavailable than others.

By that I mean that CoQ10 is not as readily absorbed by the body due to a multitude of factors. You can be receiving far less strength than the label indicates, and failure to improve may be proof of that.

For example, I have encountered many patients who came to me taking large doses of CoQ10 without a significant therapeutic effect. After drawing blood levels on these individuals, I was shocked to find low blood levels despite the fact that many of these people were taking 200 to 400 mg of CoQ10 daily. This can indicate one of two things: First, the patient may not have responded to CoQ10 because he or she cannot absorb it. Secondly, the product may be at fault. If the patient does not respond to high doses of CoQ10, the product he or she is taking may not contain enough pure CoQ10 or the product may lack bioavailability because of poor formulation or fillers in the preparation.

If the nutrient is not being absorbed, obviously blood levels will remain low. Because adequate bioavailability and good blood levels are the key to treating very sick people, I participated in two small double-blind studies that evaluated the bioavailability of several different CoQ10 preparations.[16,17]

CoQ10 Blood Level Research

Commercially available CoQ10 supplements are usually oil-based suspensions in soft-gel capsules, cap-tabs or powder-filled hard-shelled capsules, the former being the most common. While there have been many clinical studies using these preparations, there are very few reports, both in animal models and human subjects in the literature, comparing the absorption or the bioavailability of the CoQ10 in these products.

There are many CoQ10 supplements available commercially, but they are not equally bioavailable. As a fat-soluble compound, CoQ10 is insoluble in water. It follows the same pathway as do other fats that are absorbed by the body. The breakdown of fat substances requires emulsification in the intestine (with the help of bile salts) and the formation of micelles prior to absorption. Among the other factors affecting the absorption of exogenously administered CoQ10 are its particle size, degree of solubility and the type of food that is ingested with the supplement.

Although CoQ10 is classified as a lipid-soluble substance, its degree of solubility in fats is extremely limited. Commercially available CoQ10 capsules contain either oil-based suspensions (softgels) or dry powder blends. When tested in the laboratory, many of these products show a total lack of dissolution, indicating that their bioavailability is negligible and they will be poorly absorbed.

In two separate studies[16,17], we compared the relative bioavailability of CoQ10 in commercially available products, i.e., an oil suspension in softgel, powder-filled hard-shelled capsules, a tablet formula, and Q-Gel, a solubilized CoQ10 formula in a softsule (using the new Biosolv process).

These two studies, each involving 24 healthy volunteers, demonstrated that the bioavailability of CoQ10 can be greatly enhanced by using appropriate solubilization techniques. The following graphs reflect clinical studies which demonstrate the higher blood levels of Q-Gel over standard CoQ10 preparations overtime.

With Q-Gel, plasma CoQ10 values showed a sharp increase, reaching a therapeutic range above 2.5 ug/ml within three to four weeks with further increases over time.

Although the optimal dose of CoQ10 is not known for every pathological situation, researchers agree that levels of 2.5 ug/ml and preferably 3.5 ug/ml[18,19] are required to have a positive impact on severely diseased hearts. Therefore, whenever employing CoQ10 as a supplement, it is important to note not only the amount being taken but also how it is absorbed and delivered to the body.

Product bioavailability should be a major concern to scientists,

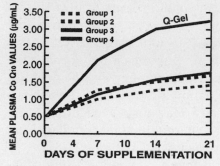

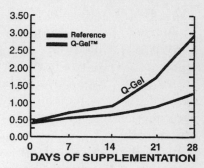

Figure 3: Mean plasma CoQ10 values during three weeks of supplementation with
CoQ10 formulations.

Figure 4: Mean plasma CoQ10 values
during four weeks of supplementation
with the oil suspension and Q-Gel.

physicians and even consumers. Bulk CoQ10 is made in Japan and sold
to various companies, but the packaging and preparations differ. New
research shows that the delivery of CoQ10 in softsules (soft-gel capsules), which are both water- and fat-soluble, is superior to the dry
form; more CoQ10 gets into the bloodstream. I am sure that as technology advances other new formulations of CoQ10 will be available
with excellent delivery systems.

Keeping delivery in mind, what dose of CoQ10 should one take?
Whether taking capsules, cap-tabs or regular oil-based CoQ10, my rec-
ommendations as of June 1998 are as follows:

- **90 to 120 mg daily** as a preventive in cardiovascular or periodontal disease and for patients taking HMG-CoA reductase inhibitors.
- **120 to 240 mg daily** for the treatment of angina pectoris, cardiac
  arrhythmia, high blood pressure and moderate gingival disease.
- **240 to 450 mg daily** for congestive heart failure and dilated cardiomyopathy.

Note: For a severely impaired immune system, as in cancer, even
higher doses of CoQ10 may be required.

Once a therapeutic effect is obtained, that is, there is improved well-
being, lowered blood pressure, less shortness of breath, healthier gum
tissues and so on, the maintenance dose may be adjusted.

I have observed that for many cardiac conditions, especially CHF and cardiomyopathy, the therapeutic dose must be the maintenance dose or symptoms will return. I have noted that some patients, well-maintained on CoQ10, will have a return of symptoms if they change the brand or the dosage they are taking. Obviously they may be getting a poorer delivery system, but if the situation is not remedied, their cardiac symptoms may return and the cause may not be recognized. Stopping or reducing CoQ10 is similar to altering intake of cardiac drugs such as beta blockers. Relapses can certainly occur.

For those using CoQ10 as adjunct therapy in treating a serious illness, it may be appropriate to ask the doctor to have a blood level obtained since blood levels are the most accurate assessment of how CoQ10 is being absorbed and delivered to tissues and organs. When CoQ10 is delivered in sufficient dosage, it will usually support the tissues in need.

PART II

Coenzyme Q10 in Clinical Cardiovascular Disease

5

Congestive Heart Failure and Cardiomyopathy

OVERVIEW

A deficiency of Coenzyme Q10 is quite common in cardiac patients. This has been well-documented in myocardial biopsies, especially in patients undergoing cardiac transplantation.[1] Researchers found the lowest tissue levels of CoQ10 in the most sick and compromised patients. Most of them were, in fact, what we call Class IV cardiac patients, those who have symptoms (extreme fatigue, chest discomfort or shortness of breath) even when they are just resting.

Because the heart is so metabolically active and requires a constant supply of ATP for continued pulsation, it is especially vulnerable to CoQ10 deficiencies. Fortunately, however, the heart muscle is also the most responsive tissue in the body to CoQ10 supplementation, rendering Q10 a nutrient with great promise for the treatment of cardiovascular disease.

CoQ10 deficiencies have been confirmed among patients with congestive heart failure, coronary artery disease, angina pectoris, cardiomyopathy, hypertension, mitral valve prolapse and even in those following coronary artery bypass surgery. In fact, the literature so well documents both CoQ10 deficiencies and response to supplementation for heart disease that in 1992 I asked the chief of pharmacy at my hospital to place CoQ10 on hospital formulary.

Coenzyme Q10 can be administered in a wide variety of clinical settings (see table on next page). Although clinical research has consistently shown that Coenzyme Q10 is clinically effective for coronary artery disease,[2-4] arrhythmia,[5] high blood pressure,[6,7] as well as the cardiotoxic side effects of adriamycin treatment[8,9] (a form of chemotherapy), over the past two decades many clinical investigations on Coenzyme Q10 have focused on congestive heart failure and cardiomyopathy.[10-17]

Potential Cardiovascular Uses of Coenzyme Q10

1. Angina pectoris
2. Unstable anginal syndrome
3. Myocardial preserving agent during mechanical or pharmacological thrombolysis
4. Myocardial preserving agent for cardiac surgery
5. Congestive heart failure, diastolic dysfunction
6. Toxin-induced cardiotoxicity (from Adriamycin)
7. Essential and renovascular hypertension
8. Ventricular arrhythmia
9. Mitral valve prolapse
10. Oxidation of LDL (prevention)

A strong correlation between low blood and tissue levels of Coenzyme Q10 and the severity of heart failure has been consistently confirmed.[1,18-20] Experimental and clinical data have provided extensive evidence that CoQ10 supplementation in patients with cardiomyopathy and congestive heart failure has resulted in improvements of multiple indicators of the heart's pumping ability, including left ventricular function, ejection fraction, exercise tolerance, diastolic dysfunction, clinical outcome and quality of life.[10-17]

CONGESTIVE HEART FAILURE

The management of congestive heart failure (CHF) and dilated cardiomyopathy (often end-stage CHF) are perhaps the most difficult challenges faced by most cardiologists today. In fact, as a practicing cardiologist for over 20 years, I have often found the medication juggling act in recycling bouts of CHF to be among my worst treatment nightmares. Although there are excellent conventional approaches in the battle against CHF, the fact remains that many patients do not fully respond to even the most high-powered drugs, and some cannot tolerate the many side effects that often occur as a result of employing them. Despite modern medicine and technology, the quality of life for those with a weakened heart muscle and chronic CHF is compromised and their very survival often remains guarded. I have found, however, that many of these individuals do improve when I combine conventional approaches (such as diuretics and digitalis) with complimentary approaches, such as CoQ10.

Remember, the cardiovascular benefits of Coenzyme Q10 are due primarily to its ability to do the following:

- Directly support ATP (energy production) in the mitochondria of the cell
- Act as a potent antioxidant
- Stabilize cell membranes
- Reduce platelet size, distribution and stickiness, limiting platelet activity

All of these actions are especially important for those who suffer congestive heart failure for which low energy output, free radical stress, cardiac arrhythmias and enhanced clotting are common culprits. Actually, CHF is one of the main indications for the therapeutic administration of Coenzyme Q10. While it is beyond the scope of this book to discuss all of the literature concerning Coenzyme Q10 and congestive heart failure, I will review for you some of the most impressive studies. I will also define CHF and cardiomyopathy as well as comment on the crucial evaluations to keep in mind when making decisions about CoQ10 dosage.

What Is CHF?

CHF and dilated cardiomyopathy are cardiac conditions in which heart muscle is so weak it cannot effectively pump blood to the various areas of our bodies. Patients with this condition usually experience fatigue and shortness of breath with minimal exertion. Fluid buildup in the lower legs and congestion in the lungs may occur. This is because the pumping ability of the heart depends upon the functional capacity of myocardial cells to expand and contract. In congestive heart failure, there are insufficient myocardial contractive forces in the heart muscle. In other words, the heart is not strong enough to pump blood out of the heart, which is why it becomes congested. The heart struggling with CHF is literally an exhausted starved heart with insufficient energy for the heart to pump.

The most common cause of congestive heart failure is coronary artery disease and the blockage of the heart arteries which can result in heart attacks. Long-standing high blood pressure, toxic drugs, alcohol abuse, valvular disease and various viral illnesses can also cause congestive heart failure, a problem which causes shortness of breath with very minimal exertion.

How Much CoQ10 Is Enough?

Although the medical literature is replete with multiple studies showing the efficacy of Coenzyme Q10 for congestive heart failure, the evaluated dose-response relationships for CoQ10 have been determined within a narrow dose range. The majority of clinical studies have investigated the therapeutic effects of Coenzyme Q10 in doses ranging from 90 to 150 mg daily. At such doses, some patients have responded, while others have not.

For example, a study published in the 1990 *American Journal of Cardiology* (AJC),[21] a prestigious journal for heart specialists, reported that CoQ10 administration was associated with an increase in CoQ10 blood levels, indicating absorption of the nutrient. A corresponding improvement in heart function was documented by the researchers. Treated subjects also reported an enhanced quality of life. When we look at the results more closely, they suggest that clinical improvement may be a function of several variables, including individual dose effects.

In this study, 126 patients (77 men and 49 women, ages 19 to 80) were placed on a treatment dosage of 100 mg of CoQ10 daily, delivered in three divided doses of 33.3 mg. All patients were symptomatic and on cardiac medications at study entry. The primary complaint was "myocardial failure" for 99 percent of subjects. Participants were followed for five years, and blood levels of CoQ10 were assessed at treatment intervals.

After three months of treatment, the mean blood level of CoQ10 in study participants rose to approximately 2 ug/ml. The mean ejection fraction of 41 percent at the beginning of the trial increased to 59 percent after six months. After careful scrutiny of individual subjects, it was reported that 71 percent of the patients achieved a significant improvement in ejection fraction after three months of therapy, but 16 percent of participants required six months for improvement. So in total, there was an overall improvement in ejection fraction for 87 percent of the patients.

Remarkably, 106 of the 122 patients who completed one year of follow-up improved by one or two New York Heart Association classes, meaning that they enjoyed a significant increase in quality of life! Only 13 percent of the treatment group did not improve. According to the New York Heart Association (NYHA) classification, there are four classes of patients with heart failure.

Class I   *No limitation:* Ordinary physical activity does not cause undue fatigue, dyspnea or palpitation.

Class II   *Slight limitation of physical activity:* Such patients are comfortable at rest. Ordinary physical activity results in fatigue, palpitation, dyspnea or angina.

Class III   *Marked limitation of physical activity:* Although patients are comfortable at rest, less than ordinary activity will lead to symptoms.

Class IV   *Inability to carry on any physical activity without discomfort:* Symptoms of congestive failure are present even at rest. With any physical activity, increased discomfort is experienced.

In summary, the three investigators had several theories for the slow responders and response failures. They proposed that the fact that 16 percent required six months' response time may mean that the 100 mg dosage was too low or that other metabolic deficiencies in this subgroup slowed the body's ability to respond therapeutically to Coenzyme Q10. At this dose, perhaps the remaining 13 percent who did not respond to 100 mg might have responded if given higher doses of the compound.

I have observed that the response window (the dose at which individuals will best appreciate clinical benefits from CoQ10 treatment) is highly variable, and often the sickest patients are so depleted that they require the highest dose levels of this nutrient. The investigators did not report the baseline CoQ10 blood levels of the 16 percent nonresponders. This may suggest that the figure could have been well below the group mean, indicating very depleted CoQ10 levels to begin with.

However, this longitudinal study did clearly demonstrate that Coenzyme Q10 is effective and safe for the treatment of patients with congestive heart failure and dilated cardiomyopathy (heart muscle disease) over an extended a period of six years.

Another double-blind, placebo-controlled crossover design study was conducted with 80 patients[11] and presented at the American Heart Association meeting in 1991. The reported improvements when CoQ10 was used as an adjunctive to traditional therapy confirmed significant enhancement of exercise capacity and quality of life when compared to conventional drug therapy alone. This study, like the one previously discussed, shows the complementary support CoQ10 affords when added to conventional medical treatments.

In a study of cardiac transplantation candidates,[22] administration of Coenzyme Q10 was correlated with corrected myocardial deficiencies and improved myocardial performance. Of 11 transplant candidates, seven patients in Class III-IV (those with the most severe symptoms) improved to Class I-II functional status (mild to moderate symptoms). In this small but significant study, CoQ10 not only improved quality of life and made it possible to extend the waiting time for a donor heart, but also justified its efficacy and safety as an appropriate vitamin supplement for patients awaiting cardiac transplantation.

A larger double-blind trial was performed with 641 patients receiving a placebo or CoQ10 in a dose of 2 mg/kg for one year. Investigators[12] reported a 50 percent reduction in pulmonary edema and a 20 percent reduction in hospitalization for the CoQ10 group compared to the placebo group. But perhaps the largest study to date demonstrating the efficacy and safety of CoQ10 for the treatment of congestive heart failure is the Italian multicenter trial by Baggio et al.[17] that involved 2,664 patients with heart failure. In this study, the daily dosage of CoQ10 was 50 to 150 mg for 90 days, with the majority of patients (78 percent) receiving 100 mg daily.

Following three months of administration, clinical improvements were noted as shown in the following chart (see next page).

Improvements in at least three symptoms were noted for 54 percent of patients. This large study is also reflective of what I have observed in my clinical practice of cardiology. There is no doubt about it, CoQ10 supplementation in patients with CHF does improve quality of life. Other investigations have also shown the positive impact CoQ10 has on diastolic dysfunction, another crucial factor in congestive heart failure.

% of Decrease	Symptom
79	Edema (fluid retention)
78	Pulmonary (lung) edema
49	Liver enlargement
72	Venous congestion
53	Shortness of breath
75	Heart palpitations

How CoQ10 Supports the Failing Heart

When the heart pulsates, there are several basic components to evaluate. Let's look at three stages that involve the ventricular muscles themselves. What we call systolic function describes the stage when the lower chambers of the heart muscle contract, squeezing blood out to the arteries. This stage requires adequate ATP energy in the cells of the heart muscle and a competent muscle to respond and contract effectively. The systolic contraction (whose pressure gradient correlates with systolic blood pressure) empties most of the blood out of the heart chambers (about 50 to 70 percent). Secondly, there is a brief moment of rest (usually less than 1/3 of a second) before the heart refills with blood for the next contraction.

This diastole stage is dependent upon energy and the ability of the heart muscle to s-t-r-e-t-c-h out without sagging, fill and accommodate adequate blood volume (about 200 to 400 ml). This entire cycle occurs in most people at approximately 50 to 90 times a minute on average, depending on the individual and the activity or energy demand.

Diastolic dysfunction, an inability of the heart to stretch and fill, is an early sign of myocardial failure despite the presence of normal systolic function. Symptoms of fatigue, shortness of breath, atypical chest pain, arrhythmia and physical activity impairment may precede the development of congestive heart failure by years. It is usually found more often in women than in men and is observed most often in clinical conditions such as high blood pressure, mitral valve prolapse and various types of cardiomyopathy or heart muscle disease. Diastolic dysfunction, or stiffening of the heart muscle, is a major cause of congestive heart failure.

Since diastolic function requires a larger amount of cellular energy than systolic contraction, more energy is required to fill the heart than to empty it. Such an additional requirement of energy activity makes CoQ10 a logical intervention. In a study of 109 patients with hypertensive heart disease and isolated diastolic dysfunction,[23] CoQ10 replacement resulted in clinical improvement, lowering of elevated blood pressure, improvement in diastolic function and a decrease in myocardial thickness in 53 percent of the patients.

In another long-term study of 424 patients with systolic and/or diastolic dysfunction over an eight-year period, an average 240 mg daily dose of Coenzyme Q10 resulted in blood levels greater than 2.0 per ug/ml.[24] These patients were followed for an average of 17.8 months with a total accumulation of 632 patient years.

Eleven patients were omitted because ten of them were noncompliant and one was dropped due to nausea from the CoQ10. Fifty-eight percent of patients improved by one New York Heart Association Class, 28 percent by two classes and 1.2 percent by three classes. This improvement in clinical function was associated with a statistically significant improvement in myocardial function documented by echocardiographic analysis which uses sonar techniques to measure the pumping ability of the heart.

It is also interesting to note that medication requirements dropped for 43 percent of the participants who were able to eliminate one to three conventional drugs. There were no side effects reported except for the one case of nausea. This long-term study clearly demonstrated that Coenzyme Q10 is a safe and an effective adjunctive treatment for a broad range of cardiovascular diseases including congestive heart failure and dilated cardiomyopathy as well as situations of systolic and/or diastolic dysfunction in patients with hypertensive heart disease. This study also re-emphasized the extreme importance of obtaining blood levels. When we know the actual blood level of CoQ10 for a given individual, we have a scientific basis from which to evaluate treatment effectiveness and clinical outcome.

The most negative and yet most quoted paper on Coenzyme Q10 was published by Dr. B. Permanetter and his colleagues, who evaluated patient response to a total dose of 100 mg of CoQ10 per day.[25] The researchers observed no therapeutic effect for their patients with dilated cardiomyopathy. However, Permanetter's study had two major design flaws. First of all, blood levels were never drawn on subjects, so baseline CoQ10 levels were never documented before and during treatment to measure parameters such as CoQ10 depletion, absorption and degree/rate of absorption. In addition, the subjects of Permanetter's research were NYHA Class I-III, with average ejection fractions of 39.5 plus or minus 11 percent (Group I) and 37.6 plus or minus 16 percent (Group II).

Class IV patients, who would be more symptomatic and compromised, were not included in the study protocol. Obviously, this was a fairly healthy group of patients. Another key issue to consider is the dose. I feel this study raises a question for further scrutiny: Is 100 mg of Coenzyme Q10 per day a sufficient dose to raise the blood level to a therapeutic window for high-functioning subjects? At what dose level/blood level do they appreciate more energy and enhanced quality of life?

The big question with CoQ10 remains, "when is the dose adequate to affect symptoms?" And, if there is symptom alleviation at a particular dose level, how soon is it appreciated and what are the profiles of the responders? How do they differ from nonresponders? What are the factors that enhance or limit CoQ10 absorption? Other nutrients? Are there other factors that may either block or burn up CoQ10? In a previous study I cited,[21] despite clinical improvement of patients, it was postulated that the 100 mg dosage may have been too low or that other deficiencies in these patients slowed the therapeutic response of Coenzyme Q10.

Another provocative question is whether or not Coenzyme Q10 therapy at this dose level provides symptomatic relief dramatic enough for someone with a much less compromised left ventricular ejection fraction function to be appreciated. We know, for example, that tissue levels of Coenzyme Q10 in heart biopsy specimens were lower in Class IV patients when compared to Class I and II subjects. This data has demonstrated a greater deficiency of Coenzyme Q10 in the most severe cases of CHF and cardiomyopathy.[1]

Permanetter also makes the statement that the dosage of Coenzyme Q10 in his study, 33.3 mg three times daily, was the same dosage which demonstrated a tripling of the plasma concentration in another study,[26] implying that his subjects probably also tripled their pretreatment level of CoQ10.

Permanetter's data was actually similar to two studies[27,28] we performed evaluating the effectiveness of different preparations of Coenzyme Q10 with varying bioavailability. Our results demonstrated that for most preparations of Coenzyme Q10, a 120 mg daily dosage often correlated with an increase in the serum level to only 1.5 ug/ml. Although a serum level of 1.5 ug/ml should be approximately three times higher than the average baseline serum level of 0.5–.6 ug/ml, research indicates that better therapeutic levels of Coenzyme Q10 should be at least 2.5 ug/ml[21,29] and preferably higher. Thus, a standard 100 mg daily dose of Coenzyme Q10 may be insufficient for some patients to achieve therapeutic serum levels. This was probably the case in the two patients discussed earlier. So, while Permanetter's study was quite thorough in the assessment of heart function parameters, the results must be seriously questioned because of the study design.

It was at the May 1996 International Conference on Coenzyme Q10 in Ancona, Italy, that I came to truly appreciate the importance of drawing serum levels of CoQ10 whenever possible. It was here I learned that, first of all, not all CoQ10 preparations can be considered equal. Obviously, absorption and relative bioavailability can affect blood levels. Even if a CoQ10 product does have outstanding bioavailability, a lower dosage of Coenzyme Q10 may still result in a subtherapeutic serum level. By evaluating blood levels, we gain direct information on how to adjust CoQ10 dosing while assessing clinical response.

Unfortunately, finding a laboratory that will perform CoQ10 levels is not always a feasible option for most practitioners. It requires special laboratory equipment and highly trained personnel, not available at most hospitals.

In general, I recommend that if patients fails to respond to standard levels of CoQ10 intervention, (i.e., 90 to 150 mg), it is optimal to obtain their blood levels for Q10. If a serum CoQ10 level is not feasible, then I would treat them clinically by doubling or even tripling the dose according to their perceived symptoms as cardiologists often do when dosing various drugs for treating CHF.

Remember, healthy heart function depends on the operational capacity of myocardial cells to generate the energy to expand and contract. Insufficient myocardial contractive forces often contribute significantly to CHF. Literally, heart failure occurs due to an energy-starved heart. Although there may be several causes of myocardial dysfunction, energy deficiency on a cellular level plays a significant role and is probably the major mechanism in pump failure. It is critically important for physicians to treat both the molecular and cellular components of the heart when managing CHF. Most doctors, myself included, attempt to support the heart muscle to pulsate more effectively with drugs, but we must first realize that the heart muscle is a collection of billions of individual cells. These cells all need an optimal supply of Q10 to offset disturbances in energy production.

Therefore, we physicians must think bioenergetically. Coenzyme Q10 has a significant effect upon electron transfer within the respiratory chain and supports intramyocardial energy at the cellular level. Because oxygen-based production of energy takes place in cellular mitochondria, it is not unusual for Coenzyme Q10 concentrations in myocardial cells to be tenfold that of the brain or colon (see below).[30]

Tissue Concentrations of Coenzyme Q10

Tissue	CoQ10 Concentration (mcg/gram)
Heart	114.0
Kidney	66.5
Liver	54.9
Pancreas	32.7
Brain	13.4
Colon	10.7

Because the heart is one of the few tissues of the body to function continuously in an aerobic mode and the myocardium requires especially elevated ATP support, any condition that causes a decrease in CoQ10 stores could precipitate a corresponding decrease in oxidative phosphorylation of the mitochondrial respiratory chain, thus rendering the tissue more susceptible to free radical attack.[31]

We must also be mindful that high free radical stress is more pronounced in advancing stages of CHF, leaving the heart even more vulnerable to lipid peroxidation.[32] The antioxidative activity of CoQ10 is crucial under these circumstances. The causes of decreased CoQ10 levels in patients with congestive heart failure may arise from the increased consumption of CoQ10 that may be secondary to the oxidative insult from the breakdown of excessive levels of adrenalin-like hormones found in CHF. This well-known increase in sympathetic nervous system activity that occurs with heart failure may also explain the increased incidence of arrhythmias as well as a worsening of heart failure itself.[33]

It has been well-documented by advanced HPLC (high performance liquid chromatography, a very sensitive and elegant method by which minute amounts of a given substance are separated and quantified) technology that myocardial tissue levels of CoQ10 are lower in cases of advanced congestive heart failure. Since myocardial tissue levels of CoQ10 may be restored significantly by oral supplementation, the use of exogenous CoQ10 should be considered not only for its antioxidant and free radical quenching activity, but for its bioenergetic support as well. Because maintenance of the body's CoQ10 stores is dependent on several factors, including advancing age, it is not unreasonable to consider CoQ10 therapy as a first-line defense against CHF. The need for CoQ10 exceeds the body's rate of biosynthesis and the small amounts found in the foods we consume.

CHF secondary to dietary deficiencies and overconsumption may be more common than we think. A recent large European study followed new cases of congestive heart failure that presented to 81 general practitioners over a period of 15 months. In 29 percent of these cases, the cause of congestive heart failure could not be determined from the history, examination and objective determinations (including laboratory analysis).[34] In this study a panel of three cardiologists determined the definition of heart failure and its cause. It is crucial to be aware that nutritional etiologies could play a substantial role in those cases that do not have clear causes for CHF such as multiple heart attacks, high blood pressure, rheumatic fever, alcohol abuse or viral insults. Because it has such a profound effect on CHF, it is reasonable to consider supplemental Coenzyme Q10 therapy for these treatment dilemmas of new-onset CHF and then evaluate the clinical response. Since diastolic dysfunction also occurs more often in women than men,[35] CoQ10 may even offer a "gender advantage" for aging women.

In conclusion, it is my belief that Coenzyme Q10 should be administered to any patient with congestive heart failure. This recommendation is also supported by a very recent meta-analysis (a statistical aggregation of eight previously published double-blinded studies). This analysis demonstrated a statistically significant improvement in ejection fraction and cardiac output, the two major physiological parameters of cardiac function.[36] Thus, an aggregate of eight studies published between 1984 and 1994 meeting strict inclusion criteria by the authors demonstrated that Coenzyme Q10 was effective in the treatment of congestive heart failure.

It is also encouraging that researchers in Naples, Italy projected from their findings that for every 1,000 cases of CHF treated with Coenzyme Q10 for one year, hospitalizations would be reduced by 20 percent.[12]

In our era of cost-containment, this is indeed a compelling forecast. The reduction in human suffering and cardiac dysfunction should hasten us to look further to CoQ10 as a first-line defense in CHF treatment based on both the clinical research trials cited and the anecdotal case studies presented earlier.[37]

CARDIOMYOPATHY: DILATED AND HYPERTROPHIC

In the discussion on CHF, I discussed dilated cardiomyopathy as a major cause of CHF. In this section we will explore the pathology of cardiomyopathy in more detail.

Cardiomyopathy is a state in which the muscle tissue of the heart has become damaged, diseased, enlarged (hypertrophied) or stretched out and thinned (dilated), leaving the muscle fibers weakened. This most often happens as a result of scarring from heart attacks. Sometimes longstanding, untreated high blood pressure may cause excess thickening of the left ventricle, rendering it a heavy, boggy and ineffective pump. Over time such a chronic strain on the heart chambers may also result in a gradual weakening of the heart, resulting in thickening and stretching of the heart muscle with subsequent ineffective myocardial contractions. This was certainly the case of L.G. (see Chapter 10), who was afflicted with chronic high blood pressure.

Cardiomyopathy may be secondary to nutritional deficiencies due to long-standing excess alcohol consumption or infections or secondary to severe inflammations like viral assaults on the heart. The heart's enlarged silhouette may be detected on chest X-ray, while echocardiograms can bounce sound waves off the heart to determine chamber wall size, thickness and contractile ability.

Other causes of cardiomyopathy may be infiltration of the heart muscle with dense, rock-hard substances that may cause inefficient pulsation of the heart. One such condition is called amyloid heart disease. Infiltrating tumors may cause a similar situation.

Frequently, progressive, deteriorating end-stage congestive heart failure may be called a dilated cardiomyopathy when the chambers of the heart become so stretched and "baggy" that the pumping ability of the heart is impaired.

Cardiomyopathy, like congestive heart failure, tends to be associated with major Coenzyme Q10 deficiencies. It may help to think of this relationship as a kind of chicken-egg phenomenon. Are these depletion states a direct result of the struggling heart's overconsumption of CoQ10 in cardiomyopathy, or is CoQ10 deficiency the major risk factor that causes cardiomyopathy in the first place?

We know that CoQ10 administration improves myocardial mitochondrial function. Most of the research findings have been reported in terms of improved physical activity, change in clinical status or improved echocardiographic studies. Recently, low-dose CoQ10 for idiopathic (of unknown origin) dilated cardiomyopathy was reported in the *European Journal of Nuclear Medicine*, 1997.[38] In this small study of 15 patients (14 men and 1 woman), only 30 mg of CoQ10 was administered for a period of approximately one month.

Investigators also looked at whether or not functional changes in the heart could be detected by sophisticated nuclear imaging. The researchers, employing single photon emission tomography (SPET), were able to document and directly measure a significant therapeutic effect of Coenzyme Q10. Their research confirmed previous findings about the clinical effectiveness of Q10 supplementation as well as the appropriateness of metabolic SPET imaging as a way to measure the clinical impact of Coenzyme Q10. It also showed even small dosages of Q10 could have significant implications for some patients with dilated cardiomyopathy.

In hypertrophic cardiomyopathy too much muscle obliterates the left ventricular cavity, causing possible obstruction of blood flow out of the heart into the aorta and arterial circulation. This impediment to blood flow results in symptoms of lightheadedness, dizziness, passing out and even sudden cardiac death. It is hypertrophic cardiomyopathy that has caused the demise of several famous athletes. Unfortunately, several of these victims did not even know they had this heart problem because they had no prior symptoms.

Recent investigations have suggested that the treatment of cardiomyopathy with diastolic dysfunction includes generous doses of Coenzyme Q10. In a study of seven patients with hypertrophic cardiomyopathy, six nonobstructive and one obstructive, all patients noted an improvement in symptoms of fatigue and shortness of breath on an average of 200 mg of CoQ10 per day.[39] The thickness of the heart chambers improved significantly with CoQ10. Using echocardiographic analysis and Doppler techniques to measure blood flow across the mitral valve also showed a nonsignificant trend towards improvement. In my own practice of cardiology I have been using CoQ10 with much success in these patients. Thus, in any type of cardiomyopathy whether it is congestive or even hypertrophic, CoQ10, because of its impact on both systolic and diastolic dysfunction, can improve quality of life.

Other Cardiovascular Applications:

Hypertension
Angina
Mitral Valve Prolapse
Arrhythmia
Atherosclerosis

HYPERTENSION

Most physicians would agree that high blood pressure is a serious risk factor for the heart. In fact, systolic pressures in ranges of 140 to 150 mmHg and diastolic pressures greater than 90 mmHg are generally regarded as detrimental to the heart and vascular system. Systolic pressure reflects the amount of pressure necessary to open the aortic valve for each contraction of the heart, and diastolic pressure is a measurement of the of pressure or resistance (to blood flow) in the vascular bed on the other side of the aortic valve against which the heart is pumping. Diastolic pressure also reflects the amount of tone in the vascular walls that "milk" the blood through the arteries. These pressure levels, both systolic and diastolic, need to be balanced: high enough for optimum circulation and energy requirements, but not so high that excess wear and tear of the cardiovascular system occurs.

The Research Findings for High Blood Pressure and CoQ10

Although the ability of CoQ10 to decrease blood pressure in experimental animal models was observed as early as 1972,[1] it was not until 1977 that Yamagami et al.,[2] documented that actual CoQ10 deficiencies in hypertensive patients exist and that the administration of 1 to 2 mg/kg/day resulted in blood-pressure lowering. Several years later, Yamagami conducted a follow-up—a randomized, double-blind, controlled trial[3] on 20 hypertensive subjects with low serum CoQ10 levels.

Participants showed a significant decrease in both systolic and diastolic blood pressures after 12 weeks of a daily dose of 100 mg of CoQ10. Several other studies demonstrated similar findings at the same dose. In many of these studies, a minimum of 4 to 12 weeks of Q10 therapy was required before blood pressure lowering was realized.

How Does the CoQ10 Lower Blood Pressure?

The mechanism by which CoQ10 brings down high blood pressure is not fully understood. However, the research of Digiesi et al.,[4] demonstrated a decrease in the resistance of blood vessel walls. This action may be secondary to an improvement in the metabolic function of the cells; the membrane-stabilizing and antioxidant properties of CoQ10 may help normalize cellular chemistry and promote optimum tone and compliance of the elastic vessel wall.

In a recent study by Langsjoen and colleagues,[5] 109 patients with known hypertension were given 225 mg of CoQ10 daily, achieving a serum level of at least 2 ug/ml. There was a significant decrease in systolic blood pressure from an average of 159 mmHg down to 147 mmHg, while mean diastolic pressures dropped from 94 to 85 mmHg. In this study, the physician researchers were able to wean at least 50 percent of the subjects off one to three of their antihypertensive medications. My clinical experience in treating hypertension with CoQ10 has been parallel to the findings of Dr. Langsjoen's work. Since using CoQ10 over the last decade, I have been able to slowly reduce at least half the cardiac medications in my patients, as well.

Treating blood pressure with pharmacotherapy is a tricky business. It's a delicate balancing act to juggle optimum blood pressure readings with the side effects of medications. In my practice of clinical cardiology, I have been grateful to have helped many of my patients lower their blood pressure without prescription drugs. At the present time, there are at least 75 antihypertensive drugs on the market. High blood pressure is a common condition in our population. The challenge for any physician is to select the best drug or medication to meet a patient's individual needs. The ideal blood pressure-lowering agent should cause no undesirable metabolic effects, be well-tolerated by the patient, reduce the risk of heart attack, stroke and kidney disease and be affordable.

As a clinician in cardiology who treats patients on a day-to-day basis, I have yet to find a single antihypertensive drug that comes close to meeting all of these guidelines. Many of my patients have paid a high price for high blood pressure control, tolerating bothersome side effects that include loss of sexual desire, impotence, fatigue, daytime drowsiness, dry cough, constipation, weakness, abdominal discomfort, lightheadedness and sometimes even depression.

Because of these serious compromises, I have never been completely satisfied with the health gains from pharmacological drugs. As an alternative, my patients and I have worked together over the years to develop a completely, natural, effective and easy-to-follow method for lowering blood pressure. My core program now includes targeted nutritional supplementation that combines Coenzyme Q10 (usually up to 180 mg daily) with supplemental calcium, potassium and magnesium. When my patients follow this program along with weight reduction, a healthy Mediterranean-style diet and a program of moderate exercise, I have been consistently able to reduce dosages of their antihypertensive medications. For some I have even been able to discontinue drug therapy entirely.

The use of CoQ10 is a pivotal component of my core protocol to lower blood pressure. Although my clinical experience and that of the researchers is intriguing, the number of hypertensive patients in the investigation trials is relatively small. Large multicentered, randomized studies should be performed to further evaluate and understand the role of Coenzyme Q10 in the treatment of systemic hypertension. High blood pressure, the silent killer that afflicts millions of people in this country, remains a major risk factor for cardiovascular disease. More research in this area is surely needed.

ANGINA

Angina is classically defined as a squeezing, a feeling of pressure or burning-like chest pain. In simple terms, I refer to angina as a heart cramp. It is caused by an insufficient supply of oxygen to the heart tissues, usually the result of blockages in the coronary arteries that make the heart vulnerable. Intense cold, physical exertion or even emotional stress may cause an increased need for oxygen, resulting in symptoms of angina. Spasm of the artery walls also contributes to a reduction in oxygen delivery. For some individuals, angina is the result of a combination of coronary artery spasms superimposed on underlying plaque. When angina is less predictable, with attacks occurring at random times, we say it has become unstable (also called Prinzmetal's angina). Basically, it comes down to cardiac economics: whatever the cause, the heart's *demand* for oxygen has outstripped the *supply*.

As a cardiologist, I use medications to protect the heart muscle (myocardium) from the diminished oxygen supply (myocardial ischemia). Some drugs work by lowering blood pressure, heart rate or even myocardial overcontractility to reduce the heart's workload and oxygen demand. Other medications, such as nitroglycerin, work directly on increasing the diameter of the arterial walls, which increases the supply of oxygen to the heart muscle. The effects of these agents may allow the patient to increase his or her activity level without provoking anginal symptoms such as chest discomfort, shortness of breath, fatigue and so on.

Most of the symptoms of angina are caused by atherosclerosis, a gradual buildup of cholesterol-laden plaque that usually progresses with age. Such blockages may reduce the flow of oxygen to the heart muscle, thereby causing the symptoms of angina. Drug therapy has a definite place in the treatment of coronary artery disease. Drugs can offer an improved quality of life in spite of the compromise of coronary heart blockages. The major classes of drugs a cardiologist uses to reduce symptoms of coronary artery disease include nitrates, calcium channel blockers, beta blockers, ACE inhibitors and blood thinners such as aspirin.

As a cardiologist, I recommend these drugs every day. However, although drugs have potential benefits, they also have variable and sometimes unpleasant side effects. Unfortunately, I have treated many patients who are intolerant to one, or even all, of these drugs. This is where Coenzyme Q10 comes in. It is a gift to cardiology. Let's look at the research on CoQ10 and angina.

The Research Findings for Angina and CoQ10

Coenzyme Q10 has been found to be effective in several small studies of patients with angina pectoris. In Japan, Dr. T. Kamikawa and associates conducted a double-blind, crossover study of 12 patients with stable angina.[6] This means that the study subjects crossed over from the experimental group to the control group, or vice versa, and were exposed to each protocol; at one point in the study, each participant received the treatment being evaluated (in this case, 150 mg of CoQ10 daily), and at another point they were control subjects for a designated time period (four weeks in this trial). Thus, in a way each subject served as his or her own control.

Dr. Kamikawa's team documented that Q10 treatment resulted in changes in three areas compared to a placebo:

- A reduction in the frequency of anginal episodes
- A 54 percent decrease in the number of times nitroglycerine was taken
- An increased exercise time on treadmill testing

There have also been other small double-blind trials showing similar effects of CoQ10 in coronary artery disease.[7,8] In one multicentered study,[7] the effect of CoQ10 on exercise duration in doses of 150 to 300 mg a day was compared with a placebo in 37 patients at several centers. As in previous investigations, CoQ10 therapy correlated with an increase in exercise duration and a decrease in the frequency of anginal attacks.

In the 1994 study by Schardt et al.,[8] 15 patients with chronic stable angina were enrolled in another double-blind crossover trial. Participants took 600 mg of Q10, placebo or a combination of antianginal drugs (beta blockers and nitrates). Results of the three interventions were compared. Treatment with CoQ10 showed a significant reduction in exercise-induced electrocardiographic abnormalities on stress testing when compared to the placebo. There was no difference on the stress test EKGs when Q10 was compared to standard antianginal agents. In this study, a reduction in exercise systolic blood pressure was seen during CoQ10 supplementation without any changes in diastolic blood pressure or heart rate.

Why exercise capacity is improved after CoQ10 administration is not fully understood. Several mechanisms are possible. First of all, there is the fact that CoQ10 has beneficial effects on oxidative phosphorylation, the process by which metabolic energy is released for cellular functions. Or perhaps CoQ10's antianginal action is the result of enhanced resynthesis of ATP, a direct membrane protection, a reduction in free radical stress or perhaps all of the above in combination. Q10's properties are certainly different actions than those of conventional antianginal agents such as nitrates, beta blockers and calcium antagonists. Although large placebo-controlled randomized trials are needed to examine the antianginal effects of CoQ10, it is reasonable to administer CoQ10 to any patients who have an unsatisfactory quality of life despite conventional medical and surgical therapy or have refractory angina.

When I treat people with angina, I usually recommend CoQ10 in a dose range of 90 to 180 mg in combination with antianginal agents, particularly for patients who have failed to get enough protection from conventional antianginal treatments. Sometimes I have even used 240–360 mg in patients who have not responded to the lower dosages. Because my patients have been able to enjoy the benefit of a more active lifestyle from CoQ10 supplementation, I believe it to be a safe and effective treatment. With no significant adverse effects, CoQ10 is an exciting additional strategy for patients with angina pectoris.

MITRAL VALVE PROLAPSE

Mitral valve prolapse (MVP) is a common yet benign condition affecting approximately 4 percent of the population. The mitral valve (MV) has two cusps or flaps and is so named because its appearance resembles that of the dual-peaked miter (or hat) of a bishop. The mitral valve sits between the left atrium and the left ventricle. The major job of the MV is to open freely and far enough to allow blood to enter the left ventricle and shut tightly enough so that blood does not backwash into the left atrium, causing an eventual back-up of fluid into the lungs.

MVP is a slight deformity in the mitral valve, usually a thickening of one or two of its leaflets that is frequently associated with a prolapse (flopping back) of the cusp(s) into the left atrium. Occasionally, an associated heart murmur can be heard with a stethoscope. Physically, what is happening is that, as blood flows through the chambers of the heart, it momentarily gets caught in the sheets of the mitral valve.

I often explain to my patients that mitral valve prolapse is, metaphorically, like a sailboat catching the wind. That is, when blood travels through the mitral valve as the heart is pumping, the blood may be caught in a billowing fashion like the sails of a sailboat filling with breeze. Sometimes, as a result of this outflow, the doctor may hear a click, a murmur or perhaps even a skipped heartbeat. It sounds ominous, but 99 percent of the time patients have no symptoms with mitral valve prolapse. A few have mild symptoms and no need for medical treatment. Most patients don't even know they have it.

MVP is more common in women, particularly after the age of 40. Those with MVP (leakage of the mitral valve) are usually advised to alert their dentists before procedures so that antibiotics may be given to prevent the extremely rare event of valve infection. (In case you are wondering why this is done, it is because bacteria—normal flora in the mouth—may enter the bloodstream through an oral wound and later settle in a valve where blood trapping may create a breeding ground for infection.)

For those patients who are symptomatic with MVP, medical therapy, such as beta blockers, can be helpful to assuage some of the distressing symptoms, particularly quick jabs of knife-like chest pain and/or skipped heartbeats. But before I use medical therapy, I usually ask my patients to try magnesium supplementation and Coenzyme Q10. Over the years I have used CoQ10 for MVP with favorable results.

Approximately 25 percent of my MVP patients have reported a decrease in symptoms of chest pain, shortness of breath and especially arrhythmia on 60 to 180 mg of CoQ10 daily. There is also early research evidence to suggest that mitral valve prolapse may be associated with CoQ10 deficiency.[9] These preliminary reports from investigations in Japan also indicate that CoQ10 showed improvement in children with MVP.

ARRHYTHMIA

Heart palpitations are probably the most common complaint that brings people to my office. Fortunately, irregular heartbeats are rarely a cause for concern; they occur in about one-third of all normal hearts.

One of the most common arrhythmias I see on the monitor are premature ventricular contractions (PVCs). Although a PVC may be experienced as a skipped heartbeat, it actually occurs earlier than the expected beat and is followed by a quick pause that feels as if a beat were missed. There are many causes for PVCs—stimulants like coffee, low potassium, alcohol, an aging conduction system, antiarrhythmic drugs, lack of oxygen, MVP and so on. The list is very long. Most cardiologists do not use drugs to treat PVCs unless the individual is quite symptomatic. Before I write out a prescription for any of my patients who have PVCs, I look at the echocardiogram. If this ultrasound of the heart shows good heart function, then I use a nutritional approach featuring CoQ10 supplementation; the research findings for this approach are impressive.

The Research Findings for Arrythmia and CoQ10

Mechanisms by which CoQ10 may act as an antiarrhythmic agent have been demonstrated in animal models. Q10, by stabilizing the membranes of the electrical conduction system, can make it harder for arrhythmias to start in the first place. It has been shown that CoQ10 causes a prolongation of action potential that can reduce the threshold for malignant ventricular arrhythmias in experimentally induced coronary ligation in dogs.[10,11]

In another experimental study of rabbits,[12] the experimental animals were given Q10 before a ligation procedure. Cellular mitochondria were then isolated 40 minutes after tying off a major blood vessel to the heart muscle. Higher levels of free radicals and lower levels of CoQ10 were identified. The effect of CoQ10 pretreatment was related to the degree of oxidative damage to the cells; destruction was reduced proportionate to pretreatment Q10 dosage. When the blood vessel was reopened (reperfusion), there was a higher level of free radical stress in the placebo group compared to the group protected by Q10. This result has implications for the use of Coenzyme Q10 in cases where there is a surge in blood flow to the heart, such as in clot-dissolving therapy (thrombolysis) during an acute heart attack, angioplasty (PTCA) and coronary artery bypass surgery (CABG).

In one study of 27 patients[13] with premature ventricular ectopic beats, the reduction in PVC activity was significantly greater after four to five weeks of Q10 administration, 60 mg/day than with placebo. Although the antiarrhythmic effect of CoQ10 was primarily seen in diabetics, a significant reduction in report of palpitations was also noted for hypertensive and otherwise healthy patients.

This study also supports my own clinical experience. Similar research indicates Coenzyme Q10 treatment for PVCs is effective in approximately 20 to 25 percent[14] of patients. Additional research also shows that CoQ10 can have an effect in shortening the QT interval (a very short time period during the cardiac cycle when the heart contracts and pumps blood) on the electrocardiogram.[15,16]

In a study of 61 patients admitted for acute heart attack, 32 subjects in the experimental group received 100 mg CoQ10 with 100 mcg selenium in the first 24 hours of hospitalization. This regimen was then maintained for one year. The control group of 29 patients received placebo over the same time period. The results were remarkable.

None of the participants in the experimental group showed prolongation of the QT interval compared to 40 percent of control subjects, who had a mean QT increase of 440 msec (about 10 percent). Although there were no significant differences in early complications between the two groups, six (21 percent) patients in the control group died of recurrent heart attack, whereas only one patient in the study group (3 percent) died and it was a noncardiac death.[15] These study results suggest favorable Q10 effects on the ECG (reflecting membrane stabilization), which may have clinical and prognostic implications during the period after a heart attack, especially in patients vulnerable to ventricular arrhythmia.

The favorable effects of CoQ10 in reducing oxidative damage while reducing arrhythmia potential at the same time suggests CoQ10 as a logical choice in acute heart attack. Arrhythmia frequently occurs in the setting of a heart attack because the oxygen-deprived heart is electrically unstable and irritable cells in the conduction system can fire at random and run rampant. To date, I know of no randomized controlled trials that have evaluated CoQ10 for the prevention of cardiac arrhythmia in patients with acute heart attack. This will need further study. However, a 1996 study[16] did show the protective benefit of antioxidants in acute heart attack; their usage was associated with a reduction in arrhythmia and even death. The same researchers are now performing a randomized trial of Q10 in patients with suspected heart attack. Since the protective benefits of CoQ10 treatment were observed in the myocardial protection–cardiac surgery data, the use of Q10 in any case of acute coronary insufficiency—whether angina, heart attack, congestive heart failure, PTCA or CABG procedures—appears warranted.

MYOCARDIAL PROTECTION IN CARDIAC SURGERY

There have been numerous animal and human studies to investigate the possible protective benefit of pretreating candidates for cardiac surgery with Coenzyme Q10. During cardiac operations, the body temperature is lowered to decrease metabolism. The body's blood supply is then rerouted onto the bypass pump so that the heart can be stilled for the surgery (cardioplegic arrest). The more limited the duration of this pump time, the better.

The supplementation of Coenzyme Q10 in pre-op cardiac patients has demonstrated an improvement in right and left ventricular myocardial ultrastructure[17] when measured by light microscopy both pre- and postoperatively. Research has shown that pretreatment with CoQ10 is effective in preserving heart function following both CABG and valvular surgery.[18,19] As mentioned, experimental animal data has also confirmed that prior treatment with CoQ10 protects against ischemic reperfusion.[10,20]

The concept of reperfusion is quite intriguing. In reperfusion, oxygen-rich blood is delivered to an area of the heart that was previously denied adequate blood flow. Such reperfusion may be seen during the cardiac procedures described. Reperfusion of the heart muscle happens when a previously blocked artery vessel is unblocked after the surgeon applies a bypass, when the angioplasty cardiologist opens up a clogged vessel or after a clot-busting agent is used to dissolve the clot of a heart attack. Once good circulation has been re-established by any of these methods, highly oxygenated blood rushes in.

But the down side is that this fresh supply of oxygenated blood is delivered under high tension as excessive oxygen is delivered to the starving tissues. All this oxygen collects electrons from the previously jeopardized cells, creating inevitable and harmful byproducts called reactive oxygen species (ROS).

This process can occur at such a fast pace that it can place an incredible oxidative stress on the tissue being rescued, setting the stage for what we call "reperfusion injury." It's sort of like throwing a life jacket to someone who's drowning and then hitting them in the head with your rescue boat.

The first stage in this complex process is the release of the unstable superoxide anion. I will explain this series of reactions in scientific terminology, which may seem too complex to the lay reader. However, your health professional may wish to have this information.

There are several potential sources of oxygen-derived free radicals in oxygen-deprived (ischemic) tissue. Enter *ingredient #1*: The most crucial and best-studied is endothelial-derived xanthine oxidase which, in tissue, is a dehydrogenase that cannot break down molecular O_2. But, during ischemia, it is the xanthine dehydrogenase from the endothelial cells that is converted to xanthine oxidase, *ingredient #2*.

Ingredient #3 is adenosine triphosphate (ATP), the product of Krebs cycle activity that provides energy to the cell. One degradation product when this ATP is released is hypoxanthine, *ingredient #4*.

Now you will remember that during this postischemic reperfusion period, oxygen pours into the cell at high tension (due to increased flow). Picture the oxygen surging in, combining with hypoxanthine in the broth of xanthine oxidase. This nasty soup then thickens with released superoxide anions and other free radicals, creating a steam that permeates the surrounding tissue with widespread lipid peroxidation and damage to cellular membranes.[21-24]

Myocardial Ischemia/Reperfusion Formation of Super Oxide Radicals

---

Ischemia $\rightarrow$ Xanthine Dehydrogenase $\rightarrow$ Xanthine Oxidase
    ATP $\xrightarrow{\text{Catabolism}}$ Hypoxanthine

   Reperfusion $\rightarrow$ O_2 + Hypoxanthine + Xanthine Oxidase $\rightarrow$ $2O_2$

The bottom line is this—the major danger when reestablishing blood flow to the heart is that overwhelming free radical activity in the early phase of reperfusion may injure the vulnerable endothelial lin-ing. Without this protective seal, endothelium-derived vasorelaxants are lost (such as nitric oxide endothelium-derived releasing factor EDRF-NO). The harmful myocardial effects of such free radical stress include denaturation of proteins and tissue edema. Ultimately, the byproducts of lipid peroxidation lead to cell injury and even death.[22] This may explain why, when a patient comes to see me weeks after bypass surgery, I find evidence of heart damage (infarction) on the EKG that was not present before the surgery, even though there was no record of any problem during the operation.

Reperfusion injury following myocardial ischemia has been extensively studied in animal models by several investigators. Naylar,[20] working with a rabbit heart model of coronary insufficiency and reperfusion, showed the role of Coenzyme Q10 in preserving an oxygen-deficient myocardium. Naylar demonstrated that the rabbit heart, when pretreated with CoQ10, was protected against both the structural and functional changes induced by coronary insufficiency and reperfusion injury.

The animals pretreated with CoQ10 showed favorable metabolic adaptations; their heart cells maintained oxidative phosphorylation and cellular ATP, healthy and integral cellular processes. Similar pretreatment of animals with free radical scavengers such as vitamin E, superoxide dismutase and CoQ10 have been shown to protect left ventricular function following ischemia.[25–26]

In the introduction to this book, I wrote about the protective benefit of perioperative (before, during and after surgery) use of CoQ10 for patients undergoing cardiac surgery. In one study, CoQ10 was administered to patients just before coronary artery bypass surgery. Their surgical outcomes were compared to control subjects who received no Q10. The CoQ10-treated patients had higher myocardial performance and lower requirements for cardiac drugs that help to support heart function while coming off heart-lung bypass.[19]

Since the heart may be the most vulnerable of all organs to oxidative stress, research is now aimed at evaluating agents with the potential to preserve left ventricular function and limiting infarct (heart damage) size by their ability to neutralize ROS in situations of ischemia and reperfusion. Oxidation is also believed to contribute to the acute tissue damage that occurs in situations of acute myocardial infarction (MI) and thrombotic stroke.[27] We are also exploring agents that have antioxidant activity to block the oxidative changes that dangerously alter low-density lipoproteins (LDL) over time.[28] Oxidized LDL, because it is part of the treacherous lipid peroxidation process that can lay the foundation for plaque formation, is a new risk factor that we need to address if we are to continue to attack the roots of atherosclerosis in the future.

ATHEROSCLEROSIS AND LIPID PEROXIDATION

Several studies have indicated that Coenzyme Q10, a lipid-soluble nutrient, acts as a potent antioxidant by inhibiting the process called lipid peroxidation (the oxidation of fats, including cholesterol and its components). Researchers at the Heart Research Institute in Sydney, Australia have demonstrated a relationship between CoQ10 and circulating levels of low-density lipoproteins (LDLs). Q10 supplementation of 100 mg/three times a day for 11 days demonstrated increased resistance of LDL to the peroxidation process. In fact, the rate of LDL peroxidation was found to increase rapidly when Q10 levels were tapered down to 20 percent of their peak concentration.[29] This data has enormous implications, particularly since the oxidation of LDL appears to be the pivotal step in atherosclerosis.

Native, unoxidized LDL is harmless. But oxidized LDL is quickly picked up by endothelial cells and systemic monocytes, laying itself down on artery walls, irritating and inflaming underlying tissue, making a foundation on which to build an atherosclerotic plaque. At this stage of proliferation, (plaque expansion from rapid growth) the oxidized LDL particle acts like a chemical magnet, attracting other monocytes, foam cells and building blocks for the fatty streak.

Byproducts of oxidized LDL are also directly cytotoxic to endothelial cells, which are so polluted that they cannot produce essential endothelium-derived releasing factor (EDRF).[22,30] Oxidized LDL, when there are platelets in its area, may generate thromboxane (TxA_2), a potent clotting factor. So it is that LDL, by its toxic effects on the cell and its potential to make platelets stick together, has the lethal potential to increase vascular constriction and enhance clotting,[22] two culprit components of plaque formation and artery occlusion.

One of the first reactions in the oxidative modification of LDL is the peroxidation of polyunsaturated acids.[31] It has been suggested that accumulation of this oxidized LDL in macrophages is the process that then drives the formation of foam cells, the key ingredients to soaping up the fatty streaks of atherosclerosis.[32] Therefore, I believe that it may be the oxidation of LDL that is the pivotal step in the process of atherosclerosis.[33] By deduction, the fact that antioxidant therapy slows the progress of early atherosclerotic lesions is suggestive evidence that oxidized LDL does play the focal pathogenic role in the physiology of atherosclerosis.[34,35]

What is it about antioxidant activity that can block this dangerous cascade of events? Vitamin E (alpha tocopherol) and Q10, both powerful antioxidants, are known to be absorbed into the LDL package, a component of the cholesterol particle. Evidence has shown that vitamin E, once picked up by LDL, can block LDL oxidation.

This has been observed *in vitro* (test tube-serum) when oxidation is mediated by transition prooxidant metals.[36,37] Other vitamin researchers documented that vitamin E supplementation increased vitamin E levels in LDL by 2.5-fold and reduced damaging lipid peroxidation of LDL by as much as 40 percent.[38] It is now being appreciated that knowing the level of vitamin E in the body may provide us a new and major predictor that can be evaluated and treated to accomplish the prevention of coronary artery disease. However, the synergistic relationship observed between vitamin E and Coenzyme Q10 is even more important.

The unique ability of Q10 to recycle vitamin E has tremendous treatment implications, especially since CoQ10 has also been shown to block lipid peroxidation.[39] CoQ10 exhibits its protective effect not only scavenging free radicals, but also by preventing the formation of oxidized LDL and boosting vitamin E stores. Some researchers believe that Q10 inhibits the oxidation of LDL cholesterol even more efficiently than vitamin E.[40,41] A significant reduction in plasma levels of lipid peroxidation byproducts was noted after CoQ10 supplementation. This observation raises a strong case that CoQ10 may help decrease lipid peroxidation in healthy well-nourished adults as well as those with arteriosclerotic plaque.[42]

After reviewing many blood levels, it has become quite clear to me that excessive lipid peroxidation occurs when there is low antioxidant protection in heart patients. In people with high lipid peroxides and high oxidized LDL antibodies, I have also observed major deficiencies in vitamin E and Coenzyme Q10 in the blood. Although some of these patients also have high iron levels, which we know may enhance lipid peroxidation, when they take additional vitamin E, especially if combined with CoQ10, their lipid peroxide levels come down. I now know that it's not enough to measure homocysteine, LDL, LP(a), fibrinogen or serum ferritin. We need also to look at free radical indicators, oxidized LDL, lipid peroxides and vitamin E, C and Q10 levels.

We need to measure these markers of oxidative stress directly so that therapeutic interventions and lifestyle modifications can be individualized to help prevent the insidious dangers of lipid peroxidation products in the blood. I believe that the 21st-century risk factors for cardiovascular disease will not only include tests to estimate parameters of oxidative stress, but will also include intervention strategies to prevent such damage with emphasis on antioxidant support such as supplementation with CoQ10 and other antioxidants including carotenoids and flavonoids.

Lipid peroxidation is not the only cause of oxidative stress to the heart. To explore this aspect of heart disease more fully, we need to look at two other major sources: thyroid excess and adriamycin toxicity.

7

Thyroid, Adriamycin and Coenzyme Q10

HYPERTHYROIDISM

In treating many cases of congestive heart failure, I have encountered some patient situations where a new onset was actually precipitated by thyroid hormone excess. The tricky thing was that, although these patients presented with full-blown congestive heart failure, they had very little evidence of hyperthyroidism. Many of these individuals failed to show typical signs or symptoms of hyperthyroidism such as weight loss, bulging of the eyes, anxiety, fast or irregular heart rhythms, irritability or muscle weakness, so oftentimes their underlying overactive thyroid was not even diagnosed. Things progressed until they ended up with congestive heart failure, complaining of shortness of breath and suffering with edema, an increased heart rate and sometimes an elevated blood pressure. Only by checking blood levels of thyroid hormone did I determine that these patients had increased thyroid hormone in their blood.

Many times I had theorized that this combination of hyperthyroidism and congestive heart failure might be the result of a virus attacking both the thyroid and heart tissue. It was not until 1996 at the 9th Annual Conference on Coenzyme Q10 in Ancona, Italy that I began to put the puzzle pieces together. There I learned that overstimulation of the thyroid gland from any cause, and the excess thyroid hormone secretion it produces, can literally burn out Coenzyme Q10. The body's metabolism is so accelerated by thyroid hormone that the excess energy production drains the endogenous Q10 stores.

When CoQ10 warehouses in the body are depleted, serious dysfunction of other organs may occur, and the heart is usually a primary target. What a shock to realize that in many of the cases I had treated prior to 1996, I may have falsely assumed that it was a virus that attacked both the heart and thyroid gland. Although a virus can cause thyroiditis that leads to inflammation of the thyroid gland, there are other causes of thyroid malfunction such as autoimmune situations, tumors and other infections. In retrospect, I don't believe all of the cases I treated of thyroid disease and unexplained heart failure were due to these viral inflammations alone—if at all. I now suspect that the majority of them were related to Q10 depletion states.

Of course, thyroid hormone excess from any cause can place a terrific burden on the heart, especially if CoQ10 stores are depleted by the increase in metabolism. When such is the case, arrhythmias and even heart failure may result. Understanding this makes a big difference in how I now treat this subgroup of patients. Screening for underlying thyroid disorder is essential in any CHF of unexplained origin. Not only do possible thyroid imbalances need to be corrected, supplemental sources of CoQ10 are desperately needed to replenish the heart.

The relationship between overactive thyroid, CoQ10 and heart function was actually studied by Suzuki[1] et al., in 1984. Their research indicated a direct relationship between cardiac performance and Coenzyme Q10 supplementation in patients with thyroid disorders.

The lesson to be learned here is that any patient with thyroid malfunction, particularly those with thyroid hormone excess, need additional supplemental CoQ10 to offset the excessive metabolic drain placed on the cardiac cells and tissues. Similar toxic metabolic stress can also occur with the class of drugs called the anthracyclines.

ADRIAMYCIN TOXICITY

Last year I was saddened to learn of the death of a dear colleague of mine. He had a form of cancer, but that's not what killed him directly. His wife told me that he had died of congestive heart failure. I felt sick about it because I knew that his premature death had probably been the result of the cancer treatment, the very thing he was enduring to extend his life. I was also distressed because his cardiac death might have been prevented. We'll never know if CoQ10 would have helped my friend, but I want to share information with you about the dangerous side effects of a commonly used chemotherapeutic agent. It could help you or someone you love.

Adriamycin is a chemotherapeutic drug used in the treatment of many human cancers. We are all aware of the use of chemotherapy in the battle against cancer. It is well-known that chemotherapy drugs are highly effective in killing abnormal cancer cells. The problem is that in the process these agents interfere with normal-functioning cells as well. We have all seen patients, friends and relatives who have been treated with such agents; they suffer with weight loss, nausea, loss of hair, fatigue and sometimes secondary infections from suppression of the immune system—all side effects of drugs that are intended to help.

But the most serious side effect of Adriamycin is its cardiac toxicity, which has caused irreversible heart failure, cardiomyopathy and even death for many, a result of the cumulative dose-related damage to heart muscle. We need to ask ourselves what it is about Adriamycin that causes so much damage to the heart.

Several factors are involved. First, by initiating a firestorm of free radicals that cause cellular and tissue damage, Adriamycin generates overwhelming oxidative stress to the myocardium. As you have read, this process can lead to damage and ultimately death of heart muscle cells. Another possible cardiotoxic mechanism of Adriamycin is the inhibition of Coenzyme Q10–dependent enzymes, which further limits CoQ10's protective function. The good news is that research has shown that by improving plasma and tissue levels of antioxidants, we may protect the myocardium against the overwhelming oxidative stress induced by Adriamycin. Let me review the results of investigations in animals and humans.

The Research Findings About Adriamycin and CoQ10

In an animal study by Kishi and colleagues,[2] the administration of Coenzyme Q10 was more protective against the damage induced by Adriamycin than vitamin E alone. In a rat model treated with Adriamycin, the administration of CoQ10 restored blood levels to within the normal range and prevented Adriamycin-induced structural changes in the heart.[3]

Human data reflect results similar to those from research in animal studies. Patients receiving Adriamycin had lower CoQ10 levels in their hearts than did controls.[4] In a small study of lung cancer patients who had normal to low cardiac function, the administration of CoQ10 had a protective benefit against Adriamycin-induced cardiac toxicity. Those patients treated with CoQ10 had little to no cardiac toxicity even though the cumulative dose of Adriamycin in the CoQ10 group was higher than in the control group.[5]

Consider, for example, a 1996 investigation[6] demonstrating that Adriamycin administration was associated with very high levels of oxidative stress and low plasma concentrations of both vitamin E and vitamin A. In this small study, the authors suggested that chemotherapy patients should be treated with antioxidants to reduce the side effects of Adriamycin. In a small study of 20 pediatric patients[7] with leukemia and non-Hodgkins lymphoma, those children treated with Adriamycin and supplemented with Coenzyme Q10, 200 mg per day, demonstrated the protective effect of Q10 on left ventricular function.

This is important data in light of the fact that it has been known that acute and chronic exposure to Adriamycin can lead to a deterioration of systolic and diastolic function of the heart.[8] The study showed the positive impact of CoQ10 on myocardial function by the use of echocardiographic serial monitoring. Not only did the study demonstrate myocardial protection with CoQ10 therapy, treatment was also associated with the absence of damage to any geographical segments of the left ventricle.

Since chemotherapy with Adriamycin can cause irreversible damage to the heart, CoQ10 prophylaxis to protect the vulnerable heart seems justified, particularly since Coenzyme Q10 does not appear to affect the antitumor activities of Adriamycin.[9]

In summary, the heart is the most susceptible of all the organs in the body to overwhelming oxidative stress. So far we have reviewed the free radical stress of Adriamycin toxicity, congestive heart failure and lipid peroxidation, all of which can cause cardiac vulnerability. But the free radical theory implicates the toxic bombardment of oxidative stress as a culprit mechanism behind the pathogenesis of many other degenerative diseases including cancer, diabetes, impaired immunity, neurological degenerative disease and periodontal pathology, to mention a few.

As a cardiologist, I have had much experience in prescribing CoQ10 for over the last decade. Many of my elderly patients with cardiac illness also have cancer, arthritis, impaired immunity, periodontal disease, diabetes and neurodegenerative diseases. When treating these patients with CoQ10 to help support their hearts, I became aware of many accidental "cures." The use of CoQ10 in these other pathological situations including the inexorable decline in health that accompanies advanced aging will be the focus of the next section of this book.

PART III

Coenzyme Q10, Aging and Degenerative Disease

8

Optimum Aging

Over the past century, the number of elderly population has increased at a rate far higher than that of other segments of the population. In 1990, there were over 30 million older adults making up 13.3 percent of the U.S. population. By the year 2030, that proportion is expected to grow by 22 percent. According to the U.S. Census Bureau projections, the population defined as the elderly will more than double to 80 million between now and the year 2050. The aging 76 million baby boomers, beginning with their retirement in 2011, will place a tremendous strain on medical resources as they exist today.

But, age does not have to be an enemy. Growing older is inevitable, and it can be an enriching experience, especially if we are healthy in body, mind and spirit and have a life purpose. The real enemies I see are illnesses like Alzheimer's, cancer, heart disease, chronic depression and despair. These are the tragedies of life.

The signs of aging range from the obvious—weight gain, loss of height, muscular weakness, memory difficulties—to the hidden—loss of elasticity in blood vessels and skin, slowing down of hormonal activity and, most significantly, cellular damage from unrelenting free radical activity. From the minute we are born, we begin to age. With the passage of time, changes inexorably occur in the human body.

The search for a unified view of aging has been the focus of much research. In my view, the most compelling theory is that of free radical oxidative stress as the primary activity responsible for accelerating the aging process. As mentioned earlier, oxidative stresses occur as a result of unstable molecules known as free radicals which, if left unchecked, do considerable damage to cellular membranes. When we discuss the aging of membranes, we frequently do not adequately describe which organs or which constituents of cells are critically at risk from the chronic, insidious oxidative stress which occurs as we age. Recent research has demonstrated that it is the mitochondria which is the target organelle for age-associated diseases.

Remember, mitochondria, the so-called power plants that provide energy for all cellular activity, are located outside of the cell nucleus and contain their own DNA blueprints with instructions for the manufacture of proteins required for energy generation. It is the DNA of the mitochondria, which is in close proximity to the site involving energy production, that is more susceptible to damage than the DNA residing in the nucleus of the cell. In mitochondrial biochemistry, the metabolism of foods yielding hydrogen ions and electrons are carried by an electron transport chain, eventually combining with oxygen using the energy to create ATP. This process is called oxidative phosphorylation. Significant wear and tear to the mitochondria occurs when the electrons can not follow the normal pathway. When excess superoxide radicals occur, degenerative changes may accelerate over time, and this damage can affect the vital activities of the cell. Some researchers believe that this theory is the fundamental cause of aging. As noted earlier, mitochondrial DNA, unlike nuclear DNA, does not have a repair system. Thus, abnormalities cannot be remedied, and the gradual wear and tear that causes physiological decline over time is what we call aging.

This inborn aging process, resulting from the ever-increasing formation of free radicals by the mitochondria in the course of normal everyday metabolism, results in free radical reaction damage to the cells, tissues and eventually to the body. It was in 1956 that the free radical theory of aging proposed that free radical reactions, modifiable by genetic and environmental factors, were responsible for the aging and death of all living things.[1]

If free radical damage, subsequent DNA deterioration and DNA mutations accelerate the speed of aging, then we can hypothesize that interventions that prevent mitochondrial production of free radicals and thereby protect mitochondrial DNA could perhaps slow aging and thus delay the onset of age-related diseases. Such approaches could consist of a life-long treatment with antioxidants such as Coenzyme Q10 in combination with a healthy nutritional program including supportive phytonutrients which can be obtained through the diet or in targeted supplements to counteract free radicals.

Normally, free radicals are neutralized by sufficient levels of antioxidants within our cells. But the standard American diet, or even a so-called "healthy" diet, is often riddled with nutrient-depleted foods that fail to provide enough antioxidants to counteract the constant unrelenting free radical attacks that occur every time we eat or take a breath. Free radicals act like chemical terrorists ravaging healthy cells when sufficient levels of antioxidants are not available to fight back. Permanent cellular damage often occurs as well as accelerated aging.

As the amount of damage increases over time, our bodies become more and more vulnerable. Our strength and vitality are slowed, silently undermined. This oxidative stress and resulting membrane destruction is the *sine qua non* of aging.

As a cardiologist, I see a wide variety of responses to the aging process in my practice. Some 80-year-old individuals appear physically to be 50 or 60. Conversely, I see middle-aged people in their 40s and 50s who look like they are ready for retirement.

Why do some people age faster than others? It is true that as we age a gradual degenerative process occurs. Yet people in every generation continue to live active vigorous lives without developing degenerative diseases as they grow older. What is their secret? Have they tapped into the proverbial fountain of youth? Is it genetic? Or, are they simply lucky? Is it possible to interrupt, retard or even reverse the inevitable decline of the body? I believe this is possible.

No matter what your age or your current health status, there are many ways to outsmart the aging process. For example, exercise can have a positive impact on growth hormone which gradually declines with aging. Nutritional and food therapies, particularly vitamins, minerals, enzymes and herbs, can also nurture our aging cells. Coenzyme Q10 is also a crucial supplement for optimum aging.

Since an age-related decline in Coenzyme Q10 occurs both in animals and humans,[2] it is logical to assume that there is a relationship between Coenzyme Q10's antioxidant and membrane-stabilizing activity and the toxic effects of free radical stress which accelerates the aging process.

For example, in the rat heart, the ability to oxidize fatty acids declines with age as do CoQ10 levels.[3] In humans, similar biochemical alterations occur with aging which may eventually result in physiological dysfunction. Consider the aging heart. Cardiologists know that unexplained congestive heart failure occurs more frequently as we approach the eighth decade of life. I have seen many cases of congestive heart failure which are probably related to an impairment in diastolic function (the stage of heart pulsation that involves filling the ventricles), which is a frequent accompaniment of aging.

Since filling the heart with blood is so energy-dependent, it is logical to assume that the aging myocardium requires additional ATP support to assist the metabolic energy demand of pulsation. We also need to consider the fact that valvular function deteriorates in advancing age as well. Any cardiologist who performs echocardiography frequently sees leakage of heart valves as well as some dilation (stretching) of cardiac chambers in the elderly. Many of these so-called normal changes that occur with aging may be related to a decline in the bioenergetic capacity of the heart. We also know that aging is associated with changes in body composition; an increase in fat mass and a decrease in fat-free mass, particularly in muscles.[4] Research has also demonstrated that a decline in metabolic rate is another characteristic feature of aging.[5]

Since aging is a complex biological process involving a progressive decline in the biochemical performance of specific tissues and organs, the potential for Coenzyme Q10 as an antioxidant, membrane-stabilizer and support for ATP synthesis that may slow down the physiological and biological decline that occurs with aging is considerable. We know, for example, that an increase in mitochondrial DNA mutation and a decrease in mitochondrial bioenergy functions occurs with aging. The supplementation of Coenzyme Q10, which supports all living cells with ATP, may retard the bioenergy decline associated with senescence and illness.[6] Oxidative stress-induced apoptosis (cell death) may also be prevented by Coenzyme Q10 by way of the inhibition of lipid peroxidation in plasma membranes.[7]

Remember, as we age, the amount of Coenzyme Q10 in the body declines. In fact, in one study of 73 healthy males, the lowest plasma level of CoQ10 was in the 91–100 age group.[8] Most of the elderly people that I see in my practice, particularly those in their late 80s or 90s, claim that they do not have enough energy to exercise or even perform daily activities such as walking.

That is why most very elderly people walk with a rigidity and a slowness in their steps. Although this may be a result of a sedentary lifestyle, a deficiency of Coenzyme Q10 suggests an impairment in energy. Many of my patients have asked me if I could give them more energy. We know that every cell, tissue and organ in the body requires a substantial amount of energy to have optimal function. Coenzyme Q10 is one nutrient that has a universal effect in promoting and supporting cellular energy at the mitochondrial level. Like NADH, this important cofactor in the electron transport chain plays a critical role in the generation of energy. Without Coenzyme Q10, cellular mitochondria cannot function. In the course of this book, we have discussed many reasons why Coenzyme Q10 can decline in the body—diminished intake, strenuous exercise or taking drugs that interfere with CoQ10-dependent enzymes. An age-related decline in brain function due to CoQ10 deficiency is yet another substantial factor.[9] This CoQ10 deficit makes elderly patients more prone to heart disease and neurodegenerative diseases. See diagram below.

Elderly patients are also an easy prey to bacterial and viral infections as a result of a decline in immunity. This is certainly the case with age-related periodontal disease. Since Coenzyme Q10 is so vital in oxidoreduction reactions, the crucial hydrogen-donating activity of Coenzyme Q10 makes it a powerful antioxidant which may have an interesting role in decelerating the aging process. Coenzyme Q10

Coenzyme Q10 Levels Fall with Aging in Heart and Brain Tissue

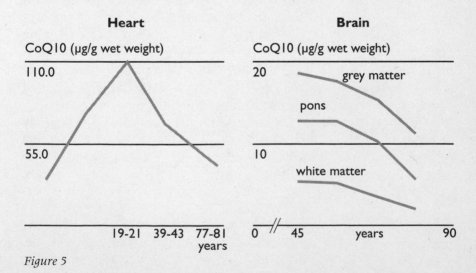

Figure 5

Source: Littarru GP. Energy and Defense, *Casa Editrice Scientifica Internazionale, Rome, 1995.*

should be thought of as a valuable investment to prevent the age-related free radical damage to mitochondria. It may be just the right antioxidant to prevent the energy production decline and DNA mutation progression that increases as we age. Thus, the supplemental use of Coenzyme Q10 may be one way to support the immune system as well as to prevent the degenerative diseases that occur with aging.

9

Immunity and Defense

Most experts in preventive medicine would agree that the integrity of the immune system is the most important defense against any disease. Basic immune health depends on the healthy functioning of the thymus gland, lymphatic system and spleen plus the germ-killing ability of white blood cells and especially macrophages produced in the bone marrow. As you may know, an elevated white blood count is a sign that the body is working to combat infection and disease, and the macrophage or so-called "killer white blood cell" plays the lead role in maintaining immune response.

Macrophages are found in human and animal plasma, as well as in more primitive life forms. This suggests that, from an evolutionary point of view, the macrophage may be one of the oldest and most competent cells, preserved over millions of years to protect any organism from outside invaders. Macrophages can be activated by a variety of threatening stimuli, including environmental toxins (insecticides or pesticides), bacteria, viruses, oxidized fats and even cigarette smoke, to mention a few.

Unfortunately, the immune system slows down as we age, which is why more older people develop cancer than young. A healthy immune system engulfs and destroys rapidly growing tumor cells when we are young. The aging immune system, on the other hand, is more often asleep at the wheel, allowing unhealthy cells to go unnoticed at times. And even when it is on the job, its ability to knock out cancers and diseases weakens with age. Many of our cells also undergo the phenomenon of apoptosis.

In apoptosis a series of changes cells undergo at the time of "programmed" or physiological cell death, cells shrink, causing altered plasma membranes and nuclear changes prior to DNA fragmentation. Free radicals trigger apoptosis in some physiological conditions, when free radical production exceeds the antioxidant defenses in the tissues. Apoptosis has been linked to several degenerative conditions, including cancer, heart disease and neurodegenerative diseases.

Apoptosis of the thymus gland is another declining immune function with age. This specialized immune tissue, found in the upper part of the chest and lower throat area, begins to deteriorate after adolescence, gradually resulting in a reduction of glandular function. The thymus gland produces important components of the immune system called "T cells." When the body loses its intrinsic ability to produce antibodies, or when white blood cell functions deteriorate, the body may become more prone to degenerative and/or infectious diseases.

Vulnerability to cancer, Alzheimer's, Type II diabetes and cataracts, to mention a few diseases of aging, occur more often after the age of 40. This is why a strong and vigorous immune system is absolutely essential for optimum health, even more so as we age. Since elderly people are more vulnerable to nutritional deficiencies, and especially since other negative lifestyle factors may also contribute, it is difficult to determine the relationship between compromised lifestyle and compromised immunity. Most people 65+ have depressed immunity simply by virtue of their age. Add to that a lack of exercise, declining antioxidant levels, indoor confinement and dietary hazards (not enough fresh fruits and vegetables plus microwave cooking, which destroys food value) and you've got the perfect set-up for a malfunctioning immune system and an increased vulnerability to infection and degenerative diseases like cancer and osteoporosis. Thus, negative lifestyle factors as well as aging can contribute to physiological dysfunction as we grow older.

We know that antioxidant levels (including CoQ10) decline with aging. This raises a crucial question. Can these low levels predispose us to impaired immunity?

The Research Findings on Immunity and Coenzyme Q10

The relationship between Coenzyme Q10 and the healthy functioning of the immune system has been gaining increasing attention over the last few years. Because the cells and tissues that play a key role in our body's immune function are so dependent on high cellular ATP production, an adequate supply of Coenzyme Q10 is necessary for their optimum health. Several animal studies performed on rodents have demonstrated an immune-enhancing effect with CoQ10 supplementation. This was attributed to an increased production of white blood cells and the increased killing activity of macrophages, the frontline warriors in immune system defenses.[1-3]

In one study of aging mice, immune system decline was associated with diminished levels of Coenzyme Q10 in thymic tissue,[3] and the addition of supplemental CoQ10 was shown to support immune system function. In another animal study using rodents, the gradual decline of the immune system was partially reversed by treating aging rats with Coenzyme Q10. The average life expectancy of a rat is approximately two years. Rats usually die of lymphomas or other types of cancer affecting the immune system. But in the CoQ10-treated rats, investigators observed healthier coats and more energy and more interaction with their companions. Although the research on Coenzyme Q10 and longevity in rodents is controversial, the bottom line is that CoQ10-treated rats were healthier and livelier and more interactive than their nontreated counterparts.[4]

Now let's look at people. In a human study of eight chronically ill patients, the administration of 60 mg of Coenzyme Q10 daily for 27 to 98 days was associated with a significant increase in serum levels of immunoglobulin G (IgG).[5] Researchers concluded that this study suggests that Coenzyme Q10 may prevent the immunosuppression that is associated with chronic illness.

Coenzyme Q10 has also shown some promising results in the AIDS syndrome, the most profound assault the immune system has had to combat in the 20th century. There is some encouraging data to suggest that oxidative stress is the major factor in the AIDS-related diseases syndrome, and that in endstage AIDS significant deficiencies in Coenzyme Q10 have been identified. Malnutrition and malabsorption are other contributing factors to low CoQ10 levels. However, in HIV-positive patients without symptoms, blood levels were not significantly different from controls. CoQ10 blood levels were the lowest in patients with full-blown AIDS syndrome only and somewhat lower in patients with AIDS-related complex (ARC). In one study[6,7] six patients with AIDS or AIDS-related complex were treated with 200 mg of CoQ10 daily. T-cell immunity increased in three patients, and five patients reported symptomatic improvement.

None of the six patients developed secondary opportunistic infections during a 4 to 7 month follow-up, and two patients with ARC followed for more than three years demonstrated no opportunistic infections. Even though this is a small study, the fact that Coenzyme Q10 supplementation did improve the immune function in these patients is hopeful indeed and warrants further research. But perhaps the most interesting potential for CoQ10 research on the immune system is in the pathology of cancer.

Canc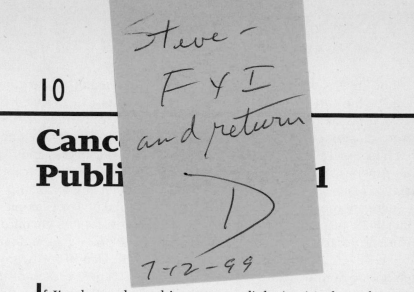
Publi 1

If I've learned anything as a cardiologist, it's that whenever you improve the health of your heart, you improve the health of your entire body. I have seen this again and again. I might be treating a patient's heart problem and all of a sudden, other health dilemmas like arthritis, memory disturbances, gum disease and even cancer would seem to improve. This should not be a mystery. The heart is, after all, the core of our being.

In previous chapters, I've written about free radical stress and the damage it can cause if left unchecked. Free-radical induced oxidative stress has been linked not only to heart disease, but to degenerative diseases such as diabetes, Parkinson's, Alzheimer's and cancer. When overwhelming and unrelenting free radical stress confronts your defenses and weakens your immune system, many of the body's antioxidants are literally burned up in the battle.

You may be asking yourself, "Why is a heart specialist talking to me about cancer?" My answer is: If your CoQ10 levels are deficient from excessive exercise, air pollution, eating nutrient-depleted foods or taking drugs that interfere with CoQ10-dependent enzymes, you, too, are vulnerable to every one of the free radical-based degenerative diseases of the 20th century, including cancer. In recent years, I have become an even stronger proponent of Q10 and am now delving further into the research on the relationship between low CoQ10 levels and cancer. There are studies attesting to the number of cancer patients who have less than normal levels of CoQ10, and there's additional evidence to show that CoQ10 supplements have been associated with tumor regression and remission.

Frightening statistics indicate that cancer is expected to be the number one killer of men and women in three years, edging out heart disease for the first time. One hundred years ago, cancer ranked extremely low on the list of dreaded diseases. Then, only one person in 30 got cancer; today one in three of us will develop it. It's no wonder that a national poll cited cancer as one of the chief concerns and fears that Americans have. What's going on? Why is there so much cancer today? I believe it is related to our pollution-ridden environment.

There are thousands of chemicals around us today. For example, if you smoke just one cigarette you are inhaling over 4,000 chemicals, including insecticides and pesticides. And then there's secondhand smoke—even nonsmokers have to deal with the dangerous byproducts spewed out by those who smoke. And that's just the tip of the environmental iceberg. Add to that the household cleaners, formaldehydes (in dry cleaning, rug and upholstery shampoos) and thousands of other environmental toxins that invade the water we drink and the air we breathe.

Stress, too, has taken its toll on our bodies, making us susceptible not only to cancer, but heart disease as well. In this century the impact of psychological stress, environmental toxicities, radiation and chemical poisons have attacked and weakened our immune systems. In fact, researchers believe that a weakened immune system will be the major health challenge of the 21st century when cancer is expected to be the most prevalent disease.

How can we strengthen our immune systems? Are there antidotes for all of this? Read on. Phytonutrients, antioxidants and Coenzyme Q10 will be the major warriors in the battle against immune system dysfunction.

The Research Findings on Cancer and CoQ10

The treatment of cancer, a disease that can be caused by an overwhelmed immune system, has attracted research into the possible application of CoQ10. In the animal model, the administration of CoQ10 has been shown to reduce tumor size as well as increase survival in mice exposed to chemical carcinogens.[1] In another rodent study, pretreatment with CoQ10 and vitamin E limited hepatic injury produced by a hepatotoxin which causes DNA damage and tumorurogenesis.[2]

In humans, anecdotal reports have demonstrated that high dose CoQ10 supplementation (i.e., 390 mg per day) has been associated with complete remission, even for patients with metastatic breast cancer.[3] In the analysis of these three patients, increased blood levels of CoQ10 were noted with a remission and reduction in cancer.

This raises an interesting question about the role CoQ10 deficiency has in the development of some cancers. It is important to remember the landmark study of patients taking HMG CoA-reductase inhibitors (the "statin" drugs) for cholesterol lowering that showed definitive benefit for women in terms of risk reduction for heart disease, their number one health risk. But this CARE (Coronary Atherosclerosis Recurrent Event) study[4] barely mentioned the nine cases of breast cancer that occurred in the almost 250 women taking the medication. (There was only one case of breast cancer in the control group.) The problem is, that while this class of drugs successfully lowers cholesterol, that's not all it does; HMGs lower Coenzyme Q10 levels by the same biochemical pathway activity. Although the investigators speculated that the nine cancers were a fluke, it is my hypothesis that CoQ10 may have been depleted by the HMGs rendering the immune systems of some women less effective. By lowering Q10 levels in women who were more at risk for breast cancer—whether due to family history, high fat diets, excessive use of alcohol or environmental toxins stored in breast tissue—this medication may have made them more vulnerable to cancer.

Let's look at the wisdom of the late Dr. Karl Folkers, a major scientist and one of the primary investigators of CoQ10. Dr. Folkers suggests that there is a biochemical rationale for CoQ10's role in the development and treatment of cancer.[5] He confirms deficiencies of coenzymes B6 and Q10 in cancer patients and reveals that abnormal pairing of bases of DNA results in mutations and diverse cancers. Because the rapid growth of mutated cells is the root of cancer, Q10's key role in DNA pathways, as well as the fact that cancers respond to Q10 treatment, suggest that this coenzyme does have a biochemical relationship to cancer.

On what is Dr. Folkers basing his opinion? In one unpublished study, he found deficiencies in CoQ10 in the blood of 83 patients in the United States who had cancer of the breast, lung, prostate, pancreas, colon, stomach, rectum and other sites.[6] The incidence of CoQ10 deficiency was higher for breast cancer; 20 percent of the patients studied had CoQ10 levels of 0.5 ug/ml and lower. The mean blood level of CoQ10 for cases of pancreatic cancer was the lowest of all eight categories of cancer. Folkers believed that the exceptional fatality of pancreatic cancer is related to extremely high deficiencies of CoQ10.

His research results were confirmed in a Swedish study.[7] Seventeen patients with breast cancer out of the 116 cancer patients studied had Q10 levels lower than 0.5 ug/ml. The incidence of breast cancer in patients with blood levels of CoQ10 below 0.6 ug/ml was 38.5 percent, comparable to the 40 percent occurrence rate for breast cancers in the United States at the same level. The incidence of low levels of Coenzyme Q10 in women with breast cancer was also reported in earlier work by Lockwood and colleagues.[3] Lockwood reported on three women with breast cancer, one of whom unfortunately had numerous metastases to the liver. Following supplementation of 390 mg daily of CoQ10, two of the women's mean blood levels increased to greater than 3.34 ug/ml respectively, a greater than sixfold increase over the average level for disease.

Lockwood's anecdotal observations of three cases reveals the need to consider high dose Coenzyme Q10 to increase the blood level to this magnitude. When such high blood levels of Q10 were achieved, clinical regression of even metastatic breast cancer occurred. Amazingly, regressions of both the primary tumor and the secondary metastases in these cases suggest the profound positive immunological activity of supplemental CoQ10.

Lockwood's experience treating breast cancer with only 90 mg of CoQ10 was ineffective and similar to my experience in treating some patients with congestive heart failure with the same amount of CoQ10. By increasing CoQ10 to 390 mg, which resulted in excellent blood levels, Lockwood saw remission in some of his patients. Again, this has also been my experience in treating severe refractory cases of congestive heart failure.

The immunological activities of CoQ10 were also demonstrated in a study by Hanioka et al., showing increased levels of Ig(G) in patients taking the vitamin.[8] Folkers measured the blood levels of CoQ10 in two groups of subjects, cancer patients and their age-matched controls. The data revealed the incidence of low CoQ10 levels to be greater in the cancer patients; none of the 38 control subjects had blood levels less than 0.45 ug/ml, while 6 of 22 (27 percent) cancer patients had levels below 0.45 ug/ml.[9]

As you can see, when we dig deeper we find that the literature consistently demonstrates that low blood levels of CoQ10 are correlated with cancer and may represent a major risk factor. At the International CoQ10 Association Conference in Boston in May, 1998 a poster presentation on leukemia in children indicated very low serum levels of CoQ10 in the majority of children afflicted. Whether low Q10 levels are a direct cause or an indirect effect of cancer requires further study; however, supplementation does raise the blood level.

Although more research is desperately needed to explore the relationship between low levels of CoQ10 and the development of cancer, the use of CoQ10 as an adjunct to conventional and other complementary therapies is justifiably based on preliminary findings and biochemical theory. And when we weigh the risk/benefit ratio for Q10, we are looking at a cost-effective essential nutrient that is virtually free of side effects.

Thus, it makes good sense to consider CoQ10 in the therapeutic management of breast cancer, especially as adjunct therapy with conventional treatments. It is also important for women at risk, i.e., aging women, women with thyroid disease or congestive heart failure and women taking certain cholesterol-lowering drugs such as the "statins" to be especially mindful about taking CoQ10 as a nutritional supplement.

The growing awareness that too many athletes eventually develop cancer also suggests the possibility that low Q10 levels may be a predisposing factor. Dr. Ken Cooper of the Cooper Clinic has been seeing a large number of athletes with cancer, he plans to conduct research to evaluate antioxidant levels, including CoQ10, in this population.[10] We can look forward to his results in the future.

Periodontal Disease

While they were taking Coenzyme Q10 to treat their heart disease, many of my patients commented that their gums became healthier. This observation is not surprising since there are many diseases which respond favorably to CoQ10 supplementation. Remember that metabolically active tissues are highly sensitive to a CoQ10 deficiency. And because CoQ10 works at the cellular and biochemical level, it helps promote strong, active and healthy cells whether they are in the heart or in the gums. What happens in your mouth is actually a mirror for your whole body.

For example, when I see patients who have bleeding gums, pus pockets, foul breath and other characteristics of periodontal disease, it suggests to me that they may have underlying heart disease or even cancer. Diseased gums may be a red flag for Q10 deficiency in the mouth and other tissues of the body. Thus, I believe that periodontal disease may be a warning sign for coexisting problems, a virtual tip of the iceberg, revealing vulnerable CoQ10 levels in the body.

This direct relationship has been observed between various degrees of tooth loss and general health. Patients with good dental health had good medical health, while those who had lost considerable numbers of teeth reported histories of poor circulation, heart disease and stroke. This is why it is important for dentists, oral surgeons and periodontists to have direct dialogue sharing their negative findings with their patients' physicians, especially cardiologists. Periodontist Salvatore J. Squatrito, Jr., D.D.S., shared the following letter with his colleagues:

I was introduced to Coenzyme Q10 by Dr. Stephen Sinatra at a hospital staff lecture. The cardiovascular system, especially the heart and the periodontium, have large quantities of Q10 in normal situations.

International studies have shown that cardiovascular problems develop with low Q10 levels. Dr. Sinatra asked me to consider the possibility of using Q10 in periodontal treatment to see if Q10 would make a difference in the outcome of periodontal therapy.

Over the years, periodontal therapy has developed a sophistication of treatment and management of contributing factors such as heredity, diabetes, radiation therapy, various chemotherapy manifestations and other conditions which diminish the movement of the white blood cells in the human system. When I was an Army bacteriologist, I developed an understanding of bacterial infections and antibiotic therapies. I tried a number of different antibacterial therapies during 30 years as a periodontist, only to be disappointed in the lasting effect of this kind of therapy. Antibiotics did not stop the periodontal disease process.

The recurrence of periodontal problems could also not be explained by inadequate plaque control. Many patients continued to be infected by periodontal pathogens no matter how thoroughly or frequently their plaque was removed. High concentrations of tetracycline gave some relief for intermittent periods of time, but over the long course, the periodontium would once again break down.

Now my patients who have refractory periodontitis are treated with CoQ10. We have been reexamining these patients for approximately a year, and have verified that the bleeding sites are diminished. The patients claim that they are still doing essentially the same plaque control therapy. The refractory periodontitis patients were placed on a regimen of 120 mg of Q10 twice daily. There was no overnight dramatic change, but we see a gradual improvement in the patients' periodontal health verified at our three-month recall reexamination. The areas that previously bled when probed no longer do so. The patients report that their mouths feel generally healthier.

A typical case history of one of the 16 refractory periodontitis patients who was treated with CoQ10:

C.G. is a 53-year-old male diagnosed as having periodontitis Complex IVA in 1982. Treatment was a full course of scaling, curettage, occlusal adjustment and osseous surgery to reduce the 5 to 10 mm pockets. The healing was slower than normal. For the next 15 years, the patient had three-month periodontal maintenance recalls. During that time, approximately every six months, he had scattered areas of recurrent breakdown treated with antibiotics and additional surgical procedures. A full medical exam with blood tests and glucose analysis were negative.

One year ago, I told him to try Coenzyme Q10, 120 mg twice daily. He presented at this three-month recall with negligible bleeding; he has had no recurrent bony infections requiring surgery and was able to go a year without more surgery. Additionally, he reported no leg pains after walking up a few flights of stairs.

I will continue to prescribe CoQ10 for my patients. Its safety is well-documented. I can only attribute the increased health of the gingiva to better health of the periodontal circulatory system due to the CoQ10.

Dr. Squatrito's expertise and clinical observations have helped us realize that gum disease depends not only on the frequency of our teeth being cleaned, brushed or flossed, but also on the state of our immune system, which can be a reflection of CoQ10 deficiencies. Basically, periodontal disease is a bacterial/inflammatory process compounded by inadequate host defense mechanisms.

Periodontitis begins as an infection at the edge of the gums. Bacterial plaque accumulates in the teeth, resulting in local destruction of the connective tissue adjacent to the teeth. The infection advances into a narrow pocket between the gum and the neck of a tooth. Bacterial antigens penetrate these adjacent tissues, initiating an inflammatory response. Gradually, the inflammation spreads to the root membrane, cement and bone, causing irreversible destruction to the bone.

With erosion of these supporting tissues, the teeth gradually loosen.

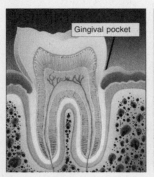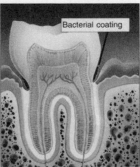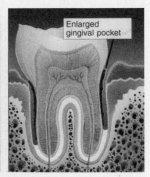

Periodontitis starts as an infection at the edge of the gums. The infection then advances down into the narrow pocket between the gum and the neck of a tooth. Gradually the attack spreads to the root membrane, cement and bone, eroding these supporting tissues and loosening the tooth to the point where it may fall out.

Research Findings on Periodontal Disease and CoQ10

Patients with periodontal disease have been reported to have lower levels of Coenzyme Q10 in their gingival tissue[1] and research has reported clinical improvement after CoQ10 supplementation.

Several studies have demonstrated that the oral administration of CoQ10 to patients with periodontal disease was effective in suppressing inflammatory changes in the gingiva as assessed by gingival index, pocket depth and tooth mobility scores.[2-6]

In an early study by Wilkinson and colleagues, 18 patients with periodontal disease received 50 mg of CoQ10 per day or placebo in a three-week double-blind trial. Clinical improvement in periodontal scores showed that all eight patients receiving CoQ10 improved, compared to only three of ten receiving the placebo.[6] A subsequent study by Iwamoto and colleagues was conducted at Hiroshima University Hospital over a 12-week period. Fifty-six patients were engaged in the study; their average age was 42. Patients in this double-blind, controlled study received 60 mg of CoQ10 a day in 20 mg divided doses. The mean score of tooth mobility was significantly lower in the experimental group when compared to the placebo group. It was interesting to note that in this study Coenzyme Q10 alone, without the adjunctive treatments of debridement and scaling, also showed improvement in the clinical aspects of periodontal disease.

How does Coenzyme Q10 support periodontal health? Most of the research in this area, including animal studies, seems to indicate that Q10's supportive effect on the immune system accounts for its ability to heal ailing gums. It is also suspected that oral administration of Coenzyme Q10 may improve oxygen utilization in gingival tissue as well as nuture the cellular membranes in the gums.

Periodontal disease is extremely common, affecting many people to variable degrees. There are detailed case histories of patients on record which have demonstrated that even the most severe cases of periodontal disease showed renewed oral health with CoQ10 supplementation.[7] However, not all the literature is supportive of CoQ10. One very critical editorial[8] with a partial review of the literature suggests that CoQ10 really has no place in the treatment of periodontal disease. Certainly when more controlled trials are performed and more objective data is collected, a scientific basis for using Q10 in a wide variety of dental diseases could be realized. For now, however, my recommendation is to consider CoQ10 for periodontal disease, especially since in my experience it has helped large numbers of patients.

CoQ10 levels fall in many disease situations such as heart disease and periodontal conditions. Actually, falling Q10 levels are part and parcel of the aging process itself. Since periodontal disease affects more elderly people than young people, it is important to consider Coenzyme Q10 as a therapeutic adjuvant in periodontal disease. Another typical aging situation is declining memory and cognitive dysfunction due to the many neurodegenerative diseases that plague modern man. We will now focus on these neurological aspects of health and the impact Q10 has on the brain.

Neurodegenerative Diseases

The role of Coenzyme Q10 in the era of neurodegenerative diseases (premature aging of the brain and nervous system) has been gaining increasing popularity, especially within the last decade. A substantial body of evidence suggests that neurodegenerative disease may be related to defects in energy metabolism, oxidative damage from free radicals and excitotoxic mechanisms causing the death of nerve cells.

Nerve cells, or neurons, have a negative charge inside the membrane while the outside electrical potential is positive. Neurons fire as a result of the influx of positively charged ions shifting across the neuron's cell membrane. If, however, the membrane is weak, too many positive charges will be allowed to come rushing across, resulting in excessive electrical excitability of the neuron, causing the neuron to fire or discharge too often. Such an overly charged neuron uses up all the supportive nutrients and oxygen within the cell; it will struggle and eventually die of exhaustion. This is one reason why nutritional support is so essential in brain function to prevent the defects in energy metabolism and oxidative damage that play a key role in neurodegenerative diseases.[1,2] Brain tissue is also highly susceptible to free radical stress since it contains low levels of natural antioxidants.

It has been demonstrated that Coenzyme Q10 has the potential to improve energy production, and may also have neuroprotective effects due to its antioxidant properties. Because of CoQ10's potential as a medicinal in neurological diseases, there are several ongoing investigations into its effectiveness.

The Research Findings on Neurological Diseases and CoQ10

It has also been shown that Coenzyme Q10 has neuroprotective effects against mitochondrial toxins. In a study by Beal and colleagues,[3] it was shown that the oral administration of Coenzyme Q10 significantly reduced lesions produced by the mitochondrial toxin malonate. In a more recent study, Beal and Matthews demonstrated that when rats were given a 200 mg/kg dose of CoQ10 for one to two months they acquired protection from malate-induced increases in 2,5 dihydroxy-benzoic acid/salicylate. This finding suggests the protective antioxidant effects of Coenzyme Q10 may interrupt the lesion-promoting effects of malonate in rodents.[4] By preventing the depletion of ATP and simultaneously exerting an antioxidant effect, Coenzyme Q10 supplementation may have beneficial effects in preventing neurodegenerative disease. Other investigations have reported that Coenzyme Q10 significantly lowered levels of cortical lactate concentrations in patients with Huntington's disease.[5]

Huntington's disease (also called Huntington's Chorea) is a fatal inherited disorder. The symptoms of Huntington's include diminished motor coordination, cognitive difficulty and depression. There have been no known drug therapies for this dreaded disease which tends to run in families due to a genetic predisposition which results from the chronic unremitting death of brain cells. The disease affects 15,000 to 30,000 people in the United States. Since Huntington's disease is such a debilitating illness, The National Institute of Neurological Diseases and Stroke has initiated a random placebo-controlled trial of Coenzyme Q10 and Astra Merck's experimental drug, Racinamide.

The study objective is to assess the ability of Coenzyme Q10 and a drug regimen to further prevent the deterioration of Huntington's disease. Participants will be selected at random to take Coenzyme Q10, Racinamide, both or a placebo for 30 months. The study is anticipated to enroll 340 people and has been named Care-HD-Coenzyme Q10 and Racinamide: Evaluation in Huntington's Disease. What I find so interesting about this study is that 21 institutions will be participating, including major medical centers across the U.S. Although the results of these investigations will not be known for at least two years, it is most encouraging that physicians and scientists are finally looking at Coenzyme Q10 as a medicinal for the treatment of neurodegenerative diseases, including memory disorders, all of which are becoming major health concerns as we approach the year 2000.

Memory impairment and free radical-induced damage to the brain is now afflicting millions of people. As baby boomers age, brain dysfunction and fading memories may perhaps become a major challenge in the 21st century. Consider Alzheimer's disease, which affects roughly four million Americans today. Approximately 10 percent of those afflicted develop the illness as early as age 40, especially when there is a familial pattern of inheritance. More often, people are stricken after age 65 as precious dopamine levels in the brain decline with aging. Alzheimer's disease, like Huntington's Chorea, is a progressive deteriorating disease in which nerve cells in the brain malfunction and eventually die. In Alzheimer's disease, the brain requires additional antioxidant requirements as there are decreased levels of superoxide dismutase, a crucial defensive enzyme for antioxidant protection. With the loss of natural antioxidant support, the brain has a higher sensitivity to free radicals. Therefore, an acceleration of aging occurs and, with impaired memory, mental confusion and severe dementia. Thus, as with Huntington's disease, implications for Q10 therapy are also being explored for patients with Alzheimer's.

In a small study presented in the *Lancet* in 1992, Imagawa and colleagues[6] demonstrated that 60 mg daily of Coenzyme Q10 in combination with vitamin B6 and iron prevented the progression of dementia for one-and-a-half to two years in patients with familial Alzheimer's disease. Nutritional support for Alzheimer's patients was also explored in a study reported in the *New England Journal of Medicine*. The study findings demonstrated that those patients given vitamin E showed a reduction in the progression of their disease.[7] It is important to understand that as we age, the brain requires nutritional support not only for the protection of brain cells, but also for enhancing levels of central nervous system neurotransmitters. Consider Parkinson's disease, a pathological neurodegenerative disorder resulting from dopamine loss in the area of the brain called the *substantia nigra*.

Typical symptoms of Parkinson's disease include tremor, rigidity, postural abnormalities, shuffling gait and a generalized slowness in motion. Although the causes of Parkinson's disease are not known, research suggests that mitochondrial dysfunction and free radical stress may be significant factors. During the aging process, not only does the human brain lose neurotransmitters, there is also a progressive reduction in levels of Coenzyme Q10.[8] More recent research has demonstrated that the level of Coenzyme Q10 was significantly lower in the mitochondria of patients with Parkinson's disease than in the mitochondrial of age- and gender-matched controls.[9] These findings suggest that neurons may be prone to mitochondrial depletion.[10] Since earlier research has shown that Coenzyme Q10 could have neuroprotective properties in the brain, the rationale for using Coenzyme Q10 in Parkinson's is suggested. However, one recent study using only 200 mg of Coenzyme Q10 in patients with Parkinson's disease, did not show symptomatic improvement.[11] The investigators suggested that the lack of clinical improvement may have been due to the limited duration of the study (e.g., three months), or possibly too low a dose of CoQ10.

Remember, the cardiovascular literature has demonstrated that high doses of Coenzyme Q10, and/or the use of Coenzyme Q10 with enhanced bioavailability may have more profound clinical effects than lower dosages or inferior preparations. The author suggested that higher doses of Coenzyme Q10, perhaps in the range of 600–1200 mg daily, should be considered for patients with more severe cases of Parkinson's disease. Another interesting observation is the synergistic role Coenzyme Q10 has with nicotinamide in attenuating MPTP neurotoxicity.

MPTP (1 methyl-4-phenyl-1,2,3,6-tetahydropyridine) is a compound which induces Parkinson's disease in animals. MPTP inhibits the oxidation of NADH (nicotinamide adenine dinucleotide), effectively interfering with the electron transport from NADH dehydrogenase to ubiquinone (CoQ10) and resulting in defective oxidative phosphorylation, ATP depletion, cellular dysfunction and cell death.[12]

Beal and colleagues, in the *1994 Annals of Neurology*[3] demonstrated that mitochondrial toxins such as MPTP could lead to slow excitotoxic neuron cell death. In their study, they used specific inhibitors of the electron transport chain which were produced by the mitochondrial toxin malonate. Their findings suggested that neuroprotection was achieved by nicotinamide, but that riboflavin administration showed no effect. They did find, however, that a combination of Coenzyme Q10 and nicotinamide was more effective than either compound alone when evaluated by lesion size. The coadministration of both Coenzyme Q10 and nicotinamide blocked ATP depletions and lactate increases. Their results confirmed the synergistic effect of using both NADH and

Coenzyme Q10 to preserve ATP which, in turn, improved cellular energy.

In a more recent study, Fallon and colleagues confirmed that the coadministration of Coenzyme Q10 and nicotinamide also blocks toxin-induced damage to the *substantia nigra* in rats. Their research findings also suggest that even a one-time exposure to a neurotoxic agent which causes oxidative stress may result in progressive neurological degeneration.[13] This is quite unsettling data and makes a synergistic neuroprotective strategy one that each one of us should consider—whether we have a family history of neurodegenerative diseases or not—to prevent the brain insult of ever-present environmental toxins and pollutants. Now, let's look at the research on NADH.

NADH

In the abbreviation for nicotinamide adenine dinucleotide, NADH, the capital H stands for the hydrogen ion and indicates the reduced form NADH. NADH and its energy-promoting cousin, Coenzyme Q10, are both extremely important nutritionals for the synthesis of ATP. Like Coenzyme Q10, NADH is a potent antioxidant with very high reduction potential to protect us from high oxidative stress. NADH is also similar to Coenzyme Q10 in that its availability declines with aging, rendering the elderly much more vulnerable to the biochemical abnormalities produced by free radical stress. The aggravated depletion of so many brain-essential nutrients make it obvious why more degenerative neurological diseases, such as Parkinson's and Alzheimer's, occur in the aging population. And remember, dopamine production falls with the aging process as well.

Some of the research on NADH looked at its presence in neuron cell cultures. Investigators found that dopamine production could be increased by the addition of NADH to the culture medium. NADH also stimulates tyrosine hydroxylase (TH), the cardinal enzyme for the production of dopamine. In a double-blind placebo-controlled study performed on Parkinsonian patients at a university hospital in Germany, patients receiving NADH showed an elevated level of dopamine in their blood.[14] Since Parkinson's disease shows a distinctive pathological pattern of degeneration of cells in the *substantia nigra*, the stimulation of endogenous dopamine production should have an effect on cognitive function, mood, sex drive, coordination and movement. So, the use of NADH as an oral compound may have promise in providing dopamine support to patients with Parkinson's disease. And, as we have seen from other research, the use of NADH in combination with Coenzyme Q10 may also give an additional boost to ATP synthesis, further improving energy production in the brain.

Since Coenzyme Q10 might help the reoxidation of NADH, this will stimulate ATP production. Supplemental Coenzyme Q10 may enhance NADH oxidation at the mitochondrial level. This would act as an electron acceptor for the plasma membrane-associated NADH dehydrogenase.[15]

The implications for supplemental Coenzyme Q10 and NADH may prove warranted not only in the prevention and treatment of neurodegenerative diseases, but also in other situations where increased energy is required. Aging, chronic fatigue syndrome and athletic endurance are just a few of the other conditions in which the synergistic relationship of NADH and Coenzyme Q10 may promote symptom relief and much needed additional nutritional support.

L-carnitine is an amino acid that also acts synergistically with CoQ10. I frequently prescribe one to three grams of L-carnitine for my patients with congestive heart failure if the therapeutic response of CoQ10 alone is not significant.

Remember that about ten percent of patients do not respond to CoQ10 alone. Adding NADH or L-carnitine may make the difference.

13

Diabetes

Like heart disease, diabetes is often referred to as a silent killer. In its early stages it rarely causes symptoms, yet it ranks up there with cancer and heart disease as one of the leading causes of death in the U.S. Today more than 16 million Americans have diabetes and about half don't even realize they have it. Each year 150,000 people will die from diabetes and its complications. Diabetes not only leads to premature heart disease but also blindness, stroke, kidney failure, impotence and lower limb amputation. In this country, diabetic complications have become the fifth ranked cause of death. In an effort to help increase public awareness of diabetes, agencies like the American Diabetic Association (ADA) are campaigning hard to provide screening centers. Anyone with known risk factors for this disorder, such as moderate weight fluctuation, excessive thirst or urination and a positive family history, should be tested to see if they have any deficiencies in their metabolism of glucose.

Diabetes is the direct result of the body's inability to break down glucose, a sugar substrate and one of the main sources of energy in the body. If glucose cannot be adequately metabolized, it spills over into the bloodstream, wreaking havoc and damage to vulnerable blood vessels and eventually resulting in eye disorders, kidney failure and heart disease. In diabetes, the hormone insulin, normally excreted by pancreatic cells, is often absent, deficient or ineffective, resulting in hyperglycemia (high levels of blood sugar), the main warning for diabetes mellitus.

In Type I or juvenile-onset diabetes mellitus, symptoms may occur at an early age, and insulin is required for proper control. Since little or no insulin is produced by the pancreas in this disease, Type I diabetics are prone to brittle forms of the disorder, meaning that they have very wide fluctuations in blood sugar and ketone levels in the blood.

These patients demonstrate classical symptoms of diabetes, such as polyuria (frequent urination) polydipsia (the urge to drink large quantities of water), polyphagia (excessive eating), weight loss and ketosis. About 15 percent of all diabetics in America today are Type I or insulin dependent.

Noninsulin-dependent diabetes (NIDDM or Type II) usually develops slowly as the result of a gradual loss of insulin secretion. It is frequently seen in individuals over the age of 40, and is accompanied by slow, steady weight gain. Usually the symptoms of Type II diabetes are milder than in Type I because the patients are less prone to ketosis. Many Type II diabetics have insulin resistance, which is an ineffective utilization of insulin. Insulin resistance causes blood glucose to burn inefficiently, resulting in excess glucose which is stored as fat. Because of the tendency to store unburned glucose, many of these patients gain weight.

Research also suggests that a significant number of maturity-onset diabetics may have mitochondrial DNA defects. Like Alzheimer's disease (which is caused by a combination of inherited and acquired gene mutations) faulty mitochondrial DNA may perhaps be the missing genetic link in diabetic expression, especially in those families with a positive history of the disease. Diabetes usually runs in families, and commonly it is the mother who passes on the legacy of that genetic trait, because mitochondrial DNA is passed onto future generations only by the mother's fertilized egg. Since the fertilizing sperm nucleus does not contain mitochondrial DNA, all of the remaining cellular material, outside of the fertilized egg nucleus, comes from the mother. In further divisions, the fertilized egg thus continues to develop containing mitochondrial DNA inherited only from the mother.

Researchers believe that one of the mechanisms of diabetes could be the subsequent reduction in ATP synthesis in pancreatic cells resulting from the impaired or weakened DNA mitochondria which are passed on. This is why diabetics may show premature aging as these faulty mitochondria are more vulnerable to free radical stress. Thus, a strategy for slowing down the aging process requires lifestyle changes and even a lifelong commitment to antioxidants to support mitochondrial function.

Although exercise programs, weight reduction and a prudent nutritional plan are instrumental in any successful diabetic management program, targeted nutritional supplements are also extremely helpful for preventing diabetes as well as enhancing immunity and supporting the utilization of glucose in the tissues. For example, all diabetics should be on a targeted program of supplemental vitamins and minerals since it has been shown that chromium, magnesium, vitamin E and Coenzyme Q10 are absolutely essential to those who have diabetes as well as to those vulnerable to developing diabetes mellitus.

The Research Findings on Diabetes and CoQ10

For example, a study done on 1,000 Finnish men[1] demonstrated that men with low vitamin E levels in their serum were almost 400 percent more vulnerable to develop diabetes. It was postulated that the Finnish men with higher levels of vitamin E in their blood were protected from free radical stress, which in turn preserved their pancreatic function. The mechanism of protective action from alpha tocopherol is that it can react with free radicals and stabilize unsaturated lipids against autooxidation, preventing the chain of events that leads to the decomposition of membrane lipids that causes cellular damage.[2] Like vitamin E, similar studies have also supported the impact Coenzyme Q10 has in preserving beta islet function in the pancreas.

The beta cells of the pancreas are highly susceptible to free radical oxidative stress. For diabetes, this free radical stress is greatly compounded whenever there are states of prolonged hyperglycemia and/or hyperinsulinemia. Overproduction of free radicals has been identified not only as a cause of diabetes but also as the culprit for its vascular complications. Since antioxidants are known to inhibit glucose autooxidation, the use of antioxidant vitamins, particularly vitamin E and Coenzyme Q10, may protect the beta cells of the pancreas by giving support against free radical damage. It has been observed that diabetic subjects have lower levels of Coenzyme Q10 in comparison to nondiabetic counterparts,[3] and research has also demonstrated that diabetic patients with very low serum levels of CoQ10 are extremely vulnerable to death from congestive heart failure within a short period of time.[4]

Since the pancreas is one of the tissues of the body that has increased levels of CoQ10, it is not unreasonable to consider that the low levels of CoQ10 found in diabetics may be the result of increased oxidative stress which in turn could be the result of an increased demand or a decreased ability to regenerate the effective form of the antioxidant.[5]

Chronic hyperglycemia is perhaps responsible for most of the long-term complications of diabetes, most of which may be caused by the production of free radicals that occurs during glucose autooxidation or glycation.

The process of glycation is initiated by the interaction of high blood sugar with the bodies' proteins. Glycation is the ability of the glucose molecule to attach to some proteins, rendering the proteins less functional and causing their deterioration or malfunction. This occurs more often in diabetics as well as in people of advancing age. Over time, glycation can adversely effect the body. It makes the arteries more permeable, allowing for lipids and other toxins to penetrate their smooth, shiny walls, setting the stage for progressive atherosclerosis. Chronic glycation also harms the precious native DNA and enhances cataract formation. Because glycation occurs earlier in diabetics than in nondiabetics, this process may cause yet another drain on antioxidants. Because decreased plasma levels of various antioxidants have been associated with the free radical oxidative stress of diabetes, it is not unreasonable to suspect that diabetics have a higher demand for Coenzyme Q10, setting them up for the chronic states of depletion that we see in their lower blood levels of this nutrient.

In a study of 120 diabetic patients, 8.3 percent were found deficient in CoQ10 compared to a 1.9 percent deficiency in healthy controls.[3] A dosage of 120 mg of Coenzyme Q7 (a molecule similar to CoQ10) was given to 39 stable diabetics every day for periods ranging from 2 to 18 weeks.[6] This treatment protocol not only reduced fasting blood sugar by at least 20 to 36 percent, but was also associated with a decrease in blood ketones of 59 percent. Since this study was done with Coenzyme Q7 before CoQ10 was made commercially available, similar results should be expected from CoQ10. However, not all the research on CoQ10 shows a favorable impact on the insulin requirements for those with insulin-dependent diabetes mellitus.

In a more recent study of 34 patients randomized into a double-blind placebo-controlled trial, patients received either placebo or 100 mg of CoQ10 each day. Insulin doses were adjusted by monitoring the patients' blood glucose. Although the CoQ10 group had a twofold increase in serum CoQ10 concentrations, there was no improvement in glycemic control; neither was there any reduction in insulin requirements. The investigators concluded that no beneficial effect on the glucose parameters that were under investigation had been observed.[7]

However, they did stipulate that CoQ10 in this dosage could be taken freely without risk of hypoglycemic episodes. Although CoQ10 failed to demonstrate a blood-glucose lowering effect or an insulin-diminishing effect in this investigation, one has to keep in mind that with only 100 mg of CoQ10, there was just a twofold increase in serum CoQ10 concentrations. Perhaps the data would have been different if higher blood levels had been achieved by increasing the CoQ10 dosage.

In 1998, a randomized double-blind placebo-controlled trial was conducted with 62 patients who had a history of hyperinsulinemia during heart attack. Participants were given either 120 mg of Q-Gel, a hydrosoluble Coenzyme Q10 (equivalent to 300 mg regular Q10) or a placebo. Those with Q10 supplementation showed reductions of their fasting insulin by 10.6 percent, reductions of their fasting blood glucose by 19.6 percent and postprandial blood glucose readings of 12.6 percent from baseline levels. These findings indicate that treatment with 120 mg of Q-Gel may improve insulin sensitivity and hyperglycemia. Since blood indicators of free radical activity fell, it is postulated that Q10 prevents excessive free radical oxidative stress. Such free radical stress causes an increase in unsaturated fatty acids and lipid peroxides due to the metabolic effect of acute heart attack and hyperinsulinism.[8]

The proper functioning of glucose metabolism is an important element in the control of diabetes and diabetic complications. Excessive free radical reactions compounded by glycation and high blood sugar levels contribute to the accelerated aging so typical of diabetes. For those with diabetes or at risk for diabetes, nutritional support with magnesium plus antioxidants, such as vitamin E and Coenzyme Q10 will help to prevent the progressive free radical stress inherent in this chronic disease.

Other Pathogenic Conditions: Chronic Obstructive Pulmonary Disease, Obesity, Skin Damage

LUNG DISEASES

Patients suffering from chronic obstructive pulmonary disease (COPD), pulmonary fibrosis and other pulmonary situations, such as bronchitis and asthma, are also vulnerable to CoQ10 deficiencies. Since infections and environmental toxins like cigarette smoke, ozone or auto emissions increase oxidative stress, the lung is a vulnerable organ to the free radical damage which can drain antioxidant levels. For example, a study done in Japan by Fujimoto and colleagues revealed significantly reduced Coenzyme Q10 levels of less than 0.5 ug/ml in patients with chronic obstructive pulmonary disease and pulmonary fibrosis. In their small study, eight of nine patients documented a diminished oxygen saturation level at rest associated with low levels of Coenzyme Q10 in the body. Investigators then administered 90 mg of Coenzyme Q10 for eight weeks and studied pulmonary function as well as exercise performance. They found an association between increased serum levels of Coenzyme Q10 levels and improved oxygen measurements at rest. Although standard pulmonary function tests showed no actual improvement, lactate production was suppressed during exercise after CoQ10 administration while exercise performance showed a tendency to increase. Fujimoto's data suggests that Coenzyme Q10 supplementation has favorable effects on COPD patients who have low oxygen levels at rest and during exercise.[1]

In another study done in Stockholm, Sweden,[2] patients with both COPD and coronary heart disease showed deficiencies in levels of vitamin E and Coenzyme Q10 in both plasma and lower-leg muscle tissue. These critical vitamin deficits may have been the result of malnutrition but also suggest depressed resistance to cell trauma.

The Swedish investigators suggested that excess free radical stress and/or malnutrition may have been responsible for the low levels of CoQ10. Malnutrition and nutritional deficiencies have long been associated with a risk for respiratory insufficiency.[3] Antioxidant nutrients such as vitamin C, vitamin E and beta-carotene have been shown to help maintain cilial function and mucosal secretion in the lungs. It is important to keep in mind that any of these aspects of physiological lung function require more optimal levels of ATP in order to promote microvascular muscular energy. Since Coenzyme Q10 levels have been shown to be low in patients with pulmonary diseases, it makes sense to consider supplementation in any individual with less than adequate respiratory performance.

OBESITY

As the director of a weight loss clinic at Manchester Memorial Hospital several years ago, I was impressed that many men and women would lose significant quantities of weight only to be stuck at a level where weight reduction became almost impossible. During these periods, it seemed that the patients needed an additional boost not only psychologically, but nutritionally as well. In these situations, I recommended higher doses of targeted nutritionals such as Coenzyme Q10 and, in several cases, significant reductions in weight loss were then realized.

Phyllis, a 57-year-old woman, came to our weight loss clinic out of frustration. She had tried several weight loss programs in the past but had been unable to lose weight. After two weeks on our program and an 800-calorie diet, Phyllis had still not lost weight. I sensed her tremendous disappointment and despair. I knew that she was really trying. After carefully going over her regimen, it was apparent that she was sticking to the diet and was even walking at least one mile a day. I suggested some dietary targeted nutritional supplements: 120 mg of Coenzyme Q10 a day along with 400 mcg of chromium picolinate plus a multivitamin and mineral complex. She took these supplements after every meal. Two weeks later, Phyllis came back with a smile on her face. She had lost seven pounds with no alterations in her diet or exercise program. Perhaps she may have had a low metabolism related to a deficiency in nutrients like Coenzyme Q10. CoQ10 supplements may help some obese individuals like Phyllis improve energy production, enhancing the better utilization of calories and resulting in weight loss.

Phyllis's success is supported by findings of an earlier study of 27 morbidly obese patients.[4] In this investigation, serum levels of Coenzyme Q10 were found to be low in 14 (52 percent) of the obese individuals. In 9 of the total of 27 subjects, 100 mg of CoQ10 was taken along with a 650-calorie-a-day diet. After eight to nine weeks, the weight loss in the CoQ10-deficient participants was significantly greater, i.e., a 30-pound weight loss, vs. a 13-pound weight loss in those who weren't deficient in CoQ10. It was hypothesized that perhaps the administration of CoQ10 improved energy and accelerated weight loss during caloric restriction. In my own clinical experience of weight reduction, I have seen similar findings, but not everyone who is supplemented with CoQ10 will lose weight. Each individual struggling to lose weight will respond differently. I hope a placebo-controlled trial with CoQ10 supplementation in patients on low calorie diets will be done in the future to evaluate the effectiveness of CoQ10 for weight loss on a more scientific basis. Since the physiology of weight loss involves so many variables, targeted nutritional supports should always be considered in addition to necessary lifestyle modifications including an exercise program, psychosocial counseling and emotional release work. For more detailed information on approaches to weight loss, see my previous book, *Optimum Health*, Bantam, 1998.

DAMAGED SKIN

The skin, the largest organ in the human body, is our most protective barrier against environmental toxicities such as ultraviolet (UV) light, ozone, auto emissions and even cigarette smoke. These pollutants, over time, contribute to skin diseases, especially cancer.

UVB or ultraviolet B light consists of short-wave radiation. This is the type of invisible radiation that reddens and burns the skin. Unfortunately, it also promotes basal and squamous cell carcinoma of the skin. UVA, or ultraviolet A, is a longer-wave radiation that penetrates more deeply than UVB but is less likely to cause burning. This type of long-wave radiation, causes premature aging, wrinkling and damage to connective tissue. Ultraviolet A may also be one of the crucial factors in the development of melanoma, the most dreaded of all skin cancers. Anyone entering a tanning salon must use extreme caution because tanning lamps emit mostly UVA rays.

Research has shown that topically applied antioxidants in the form of sunscreens as well as dietary antioxidants can reduce the occurrence of UV-induced skin cancer in animals. Studies have also confirmed that UV light depletes the skin of vitamin E, CoQ10, vitamin C and glutathione, both in the upper layer (epidermis) as well as the lower level (dermis) of the skin. When this antioxidant network is overwhelmed, there is a serious risk of oxidative damage to its cellular components.

Additional clinical research has also determined that Coenzyme Q10 is consistently the first antioxidant to be depleted in the skin. Approximately 15 minutes of intense sunlight can deplete the skin of CoQ10 levels, well before vitamin E and vitamin C are even affected. This observation was also found in ozone exposure.

Ozone is a highly reactive molecule known to increase oxidative stress in lung tissue as well as the skin. In urban areas vulnerable to high ozone exposures, CoQ10 was consumed quicker than other natural antioxidants. At the Ninth International Symposium on the Biomedical and Clinical Aspects of CoQ10, Poda and Packer suggested that CoQ10 was the first antioxidant to be affected by oxidative stress in the skin. They hypothesized that Coenzyme Q10 could be a sensitive marker not only to evaluate the antioxidant capacity of topically applied sunscreens, but also to measure the UV exposure that occurs in everyday life.[5]

Research performed in Italy also suggested that Coenzyme Q10 could be absorbed directly through the skin. When suspended in olive oil at different concentrations and applied to laboratory animals, CoQ10 tissue levels in the animals were directly related to concentration and the amount of time the solution stayed in contact with the skin. Thus, topical use of Coenzyme Q10 could be considered a form of sunscreen protection. Although more research needs to be done in this area, it is conceivable that topical Coenzyme Q10 could be utilized as a sun-protection factor (SPF).

Another new area of research is looking into the use of Coenzyme Q10 as a topical cream, not only to increase the antioxidant potential of the skin, but also to reduce the depth of facial wrinkles such as "crow's feet." A presentation at the May 1998 International Coenzyme Q10 Association Conference[6] in Boston suggested that hydration of the skin in combination with the improvement of hyaluronic acid synthesis by Q10 may be the biochemical rationale for this "fountain of youth" effect. I hope to see further investigations on skin research in the future.

PART IV

Other Considerations

15

New Hope for Male Infertility

For a couple longing to conceive a child, problems with infertility are heartbreaking. While it's beyond the scope of this book to discuss infertility in great detail, I would like to share the research that suggests that CoQ10, along with a healthy lifestyle, may play a role in enhancing one's changes for conception.

Infertility is usually defined as the inability to conceive after at least one year of well-planned attempts. This problem affects more people than you might think. An estimated 10 percent of all couples (approximately ten million people) are unable to conceive a baby. The possible roots of infertility are legion, including hormonal imbalances, anatomical problems, various disease situations, nutritional deficiencies and excessive stress or tension. The problem may originate with the man, the woman or with both partners.

For many, dietary changes plus the addition of some nutritional supplements including Coenzyme Q10, may be all that is required. These are minor lifestyle changes in comparison to some of the other high-tech treatments, and may be all that's necessary to make the body healthier and more likely to promote conception.

For instance, for men and women wishing to conceive, the avoidance of caffeine, alcohol and cigarettes may help restore the body to optimum health, enhancing the chances of normal ovulation, healthy sperm production and a nurturing environment to promote pregnancy. For women, excessive dieting or exercising has been shown to negatively impact the body's manufacturing of female hormones, so ovulation is less likely to occur. Men require a good quantity of healthy sperm for conception. Clinical research suggests that men who eat organic vegetables produce more sperm than those who eat foods that contain harmful insecticides and pesticides.[1]

Impairment in either sperm formation or motility (the sperm's ability to swim upstream to penetrate the egg or ovum) can result in infertility in men. In fact, one of the most important medical evaluations for male infertility is a complete sperm analysis that assesses quantity, form and motility. In addition, anatomical defects, thyroid dysfunction or diabetes are a few conditions that may result in male infertility. Even infections that cause high temperatures, such as the mumps, can settle in the testes and wreak havoc with sperm production for years.

If a physical evaluation fails to confirm the exact cause of infertility, such as an illness, an anatomical defect, an abnormal sperm count or inadequate sperm motility, many couples give up hope. But there are other options to explore: for example, possible nutritional deficiencies. Let's look at some of the research findings when vitamins are employed as part of a treatment plan for infertility.

Studies have demonstrated that high doses of vitamins can enhance the chances of fertilization. For example, the antioxidant and free radical scavenging effect of the amino acid L-arginine and the amino acid complex N-Acetylcysteine (NAC) have been shown to reduce oxidative stress in human semen, resulting in improved sperm function.[2] Nutritional support offers a promise to overcome infertility, especially since other studies show that simply taking zinc and extra vitamins C and E helps to promote fertilization. Now let's look at the data on Coenzyme Q10, the most powerful nutrient to enhance fertility for men.

The Research Findings on Infertility and CoQ10

Very recent research has demonstrated that CoQ10 improves sperm motility in addition to protecting human seminal fluid from free radical injury. So the mechanism of CoQ10 to enhance male fertility may occur in two sectors: first, as an energy-promoting agent and second as a protective agent. Let's consider the energy component first.

In sperm cells, Coenzyme Q10 is found in the highest concentrations inside the mitochondria of the midsection, where intense energy production occurs. Since CoQ10 is necessary for ATP production, it is directly involved with intracellular energy production. It's easy to see that a deficiency of available CoQ10 might result in a decline in sperm motility for some men, especially those who may be chronically depleting their Q10 stores to deal with free radical stress, whatever the cause.

In one study, 38 sperm samples were collected from patients with normal sperm concentration and normal sperm morphology (shape). A significant increase in sperm motility was observed in the sperm samples that were incubated with 50 uM of Coenzyme Q10.[3] In this same study, 17 patients with low fertilization rates were also treated with oral CoQ10. They took 60 mg a day for a mean of 103 days. Although no significant change was noted in most sperm parameters, there was a significant improvement noted in fertilization rates.

This important study sparked interesting speculations about how CoQ10 improves some sperm parameters in selective patients. Additional research has observed a direct correlation between CoQ10 concentrations and sperm motility.[4] In other words, the higher the blood levels of CoQ10, the greater the sperm's ability to be a strong swimmer.

Previous research had demonstrated that sperm motility, because it relies on additional energy, may actually be dependent upon the bioenergetic functions of Coenzyme Q10.[5] Since sperm motility is such an important factor in fertilization, it is reasonable to consider that CoQ10 is a key player to support the ATP activity necessary to increase sperm activity. This offers new hope for many who have failed to respond to the best efforts that the usual medical treatments offer to increase sperm motility. In addition to promoting energy for the sperms' production and their swimming prowess, we must also remember that sperm, like any biologic tissue, is also sensitive to oxidative stress—another good reason to supplement with Coenzyme Q10.

The antioxidant function of CoQ10 is another important consideration when addressing the male fertility factor.[6] Since the reduced form of CoQ10 acts as a powerful antioxidant, lipid peroxidation in all of one's biological membranes can be reduced by this vitamin. Other investigations show an improvement in several biological parameters for sperm both before and after treatment with Coenzyme Q10.[7] It is most likely that the enhanced bioenergetic effect is boosted by the antioxidant capabilities of CoQ10 that prevent the lipid peroxidation that can impair cell functioning.

It is known that defective sperm function in infertile men is directly associated with increased free radical stress. Since previous research showed that vitamin E supported sperm function even after excessive induced free radical stress,[8] it is reasonable to suspect that there is definitely a more direct connection between infertility and oxidative stress. In a recent study, lowering the subjects' free radical indices correlated with a higher fertilization rate when men were treated with 200 IU of vitamin E a day for three months.[9]

Since testicular tissue and sperm viability are both particularly vulnerable to the assaults and injuries from reactive oxygen species (ROS), the antioxidant support of CoQ10 is vital to prevent excessive lipid peroxidation in the tissues that produce healthy sperm cells. I strongly believe that the potential implications for the therapeutic role of Coenzyme Q10 for those who struggle with infertility is a solution that must be considered. And there's even more evidence for this position.

In one very recent study,[10] the concentration of lipid hydroperoxides (a measure of free radical injury) in total seminal fluid and in seminal plasma was measured. When the data was analyzed statistically, a linear regression curve emerged that expressed the relationship between CoQ10 content and hydroperoxide levels in seminal fluid. The shape of the graph (see below) indicates that the higher CoQ10 content in the seminal fluid and plasma, the lower the levels of hydroperoxide formation. The results of this study suggest that CoQ10 inhibits hydroperoxide formation in human seminal fluid. Since excessive free radical stress is an important factor effecting male infertility, CoQ10 could play a significant role in protecting patients whose seminal fluid and seminal plasma levels of oxidative stress are elevated.

As you can see, various lines of research have repeatedly demonstrated that CoQ10's protective function encompasses not only bioenergetic support, but powerful antioxidant defenses as well, and that these benefits can actually affect the level of male potential for conception. Although further investigation is needed to explore the relationship among sperm function, oxidative stress and impaired antioxidant defense, the supplemental administration of CoQ10 is a logical approach for the treatment of male infertility.

To summarize, targeted nutritional supplementation with CoQ10 as well as vitamins C and E and the mineral zinc, plus amino acids such as NAC and L-arginine, should be considered for any male with impaired reproductive function. Add a little romance to this nutrient prescription and the reward of fertility may be realized.

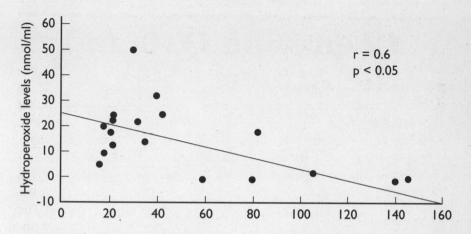

Figure 7: Linear regression between ubiquinol-10 content and hydroperoxide levels in seminal fluid (r =0.6; p = 0.02).

Reprinted from Alleva, R. et al. The protective role of ubiquinol-10 against formation of lipid hydroperoxides in human seminal fluid. *Mole. Aspects Med.* 1997; 18(suppl):s221 – s228, with permission from Elsevier Science.

Coenzyme Q10 and the Athlete

Consider this question: Why do some young athletes develop heart disease and cancer? After all, as a group, athletes are exceptionally healthy people. And yet, we often hear of famous Olympic athletes, world-class skaters, baseball players and football players developing heart disease and various cancers at a very young age.

It's actually not so difficult to understand when you consider what happens to the body when it undergoes rigorous and regular athletic training. Such training sets competitive athletes or even weekend warriors up for "catabolic stress," whereby tissues are constantly broken down.

When this repetitive wear and tear that causes tissue damage is coupled with the increased oxygen consumption that occurs during exercise, an increase in the production of free radicals occurs. Over time, these free radicals can cause damage to our blood vessels.

Fortunately, the body produces natural antioxidant defenses which can protect us against the toxic breakdown products of oxygen. It is only when natural antioxidant defenses become overwhelmed that the onslaught of free radicals can be dangerous to health. Many athletes are on vitamin E–deficient, low-fat diets that focus on consuming lots of protein with a minimal intake of fresh fruits, vegetables and phytonutrients. When these nutritionally depleted diets are combined with excessive free radical production, a syndrome of antioxidant insufficiency often occurs. This explains why some marathon runners, in apparently peak physical condition, develop early and premature coronary heart disease.

Nearly 20 years ago, as a fellow in cardiology, I was horrified by a study of sudden death in marathon runners.[1] Six asymptomatic men in their 40s all died while running. Their autopsy reports demonstrated far-advanced coronary artery disease. It wasn't until years later, after doing much research in antioxidants and phytonutrients, that I realized that the chronic wear and tear on their poorly nourished bodies resulted in such an extreme antioxidant insufficiency that the unchallenged free radical stress caused premature heart disease and death. Moreover, when athletes run in polluted environments with excessive ozone and auto emissions, even more oxidative stress occurs in the tissues.

Exercise-induced free radicals can contribute to the development of arterial blockage. These excess free radicals can enhance the oxidation of LDL cholesterol, which sticks to the walls of the arteries in the form of plaque. Over time, such a tremendous, repeated influx of excessive free radical stress can set the stage for coronary disease. I am sure this was the reason why the six marathon runners developed premature heart disease. One of them had participated in six marathons and was in great physical shape, but suddenly dropped dead during his seventh marathon. His autopsy revealed that the condition of his heart was similar to the hearts of people who suffer fatal heart attacks due to severe arteriosclerotic heart disease.

How can you protect yourself if you are an athlete, marathon runner or even a weekend warrior? Extensive research indicates that antioxidant supplements neutralize free radicals before they can do their damage by preventing the oxidation of fats and by stabilizing cell membranes before they are broken down by exercise. Since clinical studies have also shown that antioxidant levels are low for both exercising animals and humans, it makes sense to take antioxidant supplements regularly prior to exercise.

In one study, for example, CoQ10 and vitamin E levels were analyzed in healthy sedentary male subjects, endurance-trained male athletes and patients with severe coronary heart disease. Higher CoQ10 levels were found in sedentary male subjects compared to both the heart patients and the endurance-trained athletes. The researchers speculated that with such high metabolic stress and elevated free radical formation in marathon runners, lower CoQ10 and vitamin E levels were reflective of a continuing drain on their antioxidant scavenging potential.[2] Similar findings in recreational sports were also noted in another investigation.

In a recent study performed in a small Mediterranean town, investigators found that people performing highly aerobic activities, such as jogging, biking and other sports, had lower levels of circulating antioxidants, particularly CoQ10 and vitamin E.[3]

Gian Paolo Littarru reported data on physical exercise, free radicals and Coenzyme Q10 in his excellent book *Energy and Defense*.[4] Littarru also confirms that early studies have demonstrated low plasma CoQ10 levels in athletes when compared to normal sedentary controls of the same age. Littarru revealed that these low CoQ10 levels are the result of dynamic imbalances. He states that although the biosynthesis of CoQ10 in athletes is probably more elevated, metabolism and breakdown processes are also geared up higher. This accelerated turnover would lead to a more rapid uptake of CoQ10 in muscular tissue, thus resulting in lower blood levels. Data seems to indicate that athletic training accompanied by an increase in oxidative stress stimulates the synthesis of CoQ10 in order to meet the increased demands for antioxidant protection.

It is intriguing to speculate whether the administration of CoQ10 is capable of attenuating oxidative damage. Experimental animal data has shed some light on this hypothesis. In a study in rats, the animals receiving Coenzyme Q10 showed a decrease in the initial release of muscle breakdown products, suggesting that CoQ10 supports muscular membranes and reduces tissue damage from excessive free radical oxidative stress.[5] Similar findings were also noted in an experiment conducted on athletes.

Marathon runners pretreated with Coenzyme Q10 had lower plasma levels of tissue breakdown products and enzymes compared to their controlled counterparts.[6] Although the mechanism of tissue injuries in athletes is very complex and other factors may be working other than the role played by free radicals, the fact that athletes do have lower tissue levels of antioxidants is intriguing. Although antioxidant support can offer protection to athletes from free radical stress, the other question we need to ask is: Can Coenzyme Q10 also increase performance and endurance?

The promise that Coenzyme Q10 supplements offers for exercise endurance and/or performance has perhaps been one of the most controversial and argued aspects about this nutrient. The literature has also been controversial; some studies have supported and some studies have refuted positive correlations between Coenzyme Q10 supplementation and exercise performance. There is, however, some agreement that enhancing exercise performance and endurance may be helpful for the small subsets of patients who suffer from muscular dystrophy and may also offer improved muscle function for patients who have chronic obstructive pulmonary disease. For now, I will try to give you both sides of the argument by presenting examples of both the positive and negative research.

Since CoQ10 is a powerful antioxidant and is also involved in energy production, could the supplemental addition of CoQ10 enhance aerobic capacity and improve muscle performance? In 1981, there was a small study of six healthy men who were not used to doing any type of exercise. They were given CoQ10, 60 mg every day for eight weeks. A bicycle ergometer test was performed before and after the CoQ10 supplementation period. The second test showed slight improved performance including work capacity, oxygen consumption and oxygen transport.[7] Although these improvements only ranged from 3–12 percent, the study did suggest that the use of supplementary CoQ10 could, perhaps, improve physical performance. Since that time, multiple studies have been performed with controversial results.

The effect of Coenzyme Q10 on exercise performance was studied in a double-blind crossover trial of 25 Finnish top-level cross-country skiers. After their supplemental period, 94 percent of the athletes felt that Coenzyme Q10 had been beneficial in improving their performance and recovery time compared to 33 percent of the skiers on placebo intervention who felt their performance was improved.[8] It was also interesting to note that with CoQ10 administration, all measured indices of physical performance, including VO_2 Max (a measurement of oxygen capacity at maximal point of exertion), improved significantly. This is significant because as VO_2 Max increases, the total performance capacity also increases. Thus, athletes can train harder and more intensively, increasing their workouts and thus probably maximizing their physical performance. In this study, with the supplemental administration of the Pharma nord brand of CoQ10, 90 mg per day, physical performance capacity improved after six weeks, probably due to Q10-induced changes in energy production. It should also be mentioned that a threefold increase in blood concentrations of CoQ10 was realized in the treated skiers.

However, all the findings on Q10 and exercise have not been positive. In a more recent study, the effect of orally supplemented Coenzyme Q10 on plasma CoQ10 concentration and aerobic capacity in endurance-trained athletes failed to show any significant effects on parameters of oxygen uptake, aerobic capacity or respiratory compensation threshold after graded cycling to exhaustion.[9] Important to note is that plasma CoQ10 concentrations, for the most part, were only two times above baseline levels.[8] We can only speculate that positive responses might have been observed if Q10 blood concentrations were higher, as was documented in the previous study of cross-country skiers.

In another study performed at Wayne State University, Porter and colleagues[10] determined that the effect of oral CoQ10 dosing on exercise capacity for 15 middle-aged men who received 150 mg of CoQ10 or placebo for a two-month period. Although blood levels increased in this study from pretreatment average of 0.72 ug/ml to a posttreatment average of 1.08 ug/ml, again a substantial blood level was not realized. This study, like the previous negative report, concluded that the short-term administration of CoQ10 did not improve maximal oxygen consumption and aerobic capacity in middle-aged untrained men. However, it was also interesting to note that the subjective perception of increased vigor was appreciated more by the men with the slightly higher blood levels of CoQ10.

In another investigation,[11] a cocktail of 100 mg of CoQ10, 500 mg of vitamin C and 200 IU of vitamin E was administered to 11 highly trained athletes for two four-week periods using a double-blind crossover design. A grueling performance test consisting of 90 minutes of running on a treadmill followed by cycling until exhaustion was conducted after each treatment period. Metabolic parameters of free fatty-acid concentrations, blood glucose and lactate did not differ between the groups. However, again we have to ask ourselves the question: Is the 100 mg dose or the delivery system capable of raising the blood level to a substantial enough level that will influence performance? This is the most critical point we must consider.

In comparing these studies, it appears that significant improvements in objective and subjective parameters in exercise endurance are directly related to higher blood levels of CoQ10. Again, this has been my personal clinical experience in treating congestive heart failure with CoQ10.[10] If the most critically ill patients frequently fail to show improvement of symptoms at lower blood levels, could the same be true for athletes? In order for CoQ10 to increase endurance, it is imperative that it penetrate into the mitochondria to enhance ATP production. Do higher blood levels insure that CoQ10 is being absorbed into mito-chondria more easily? I believe the issue of mitochondrial dynamics in athletes should be the focus of future investigations.

For now, given all the controversial data, I would certainly recom-mend the equivalent of at least 200 to 300 mg of daily Coenzyme Q10 supplementation for athletes. Since there is agreement demonstrating lower plasma levels of CoQ10 in this population, it seems prudent and wise to consider supplementation.

Muscular Dystrophy and Mitochondrial Encephalopathy

MUSCULAR DYSTROPHY

Many of us rally to the aid of Jerry Lewis and his telethon to raise funds for more research into muscular dystrophies (MD). The children and adults who struggle with the limitations of these crippling disorders touch our hearts and move us to help with our donations.

Muscular dystrophies are inherited muscle diseases characterized by severe progressive weakness. Fortunately, the muscular dystrophies of the Duchenne, facioscapulohumeral, limb-girdle and myotonic dystrophy type are not common. About two-thirds of these cases appear sporadically with no other affected individuals in an MD patient's family. These tragic human muscular disorders involve pathological abnormalities that are usually restricted to skeletal muscle but frequently involve cardiac muscle as well. Usually the brain, spinal cord, and peripheral nerves are not affected with metabolic or histological changes (those that we can see with a microscope).

The abnormalities of MD involve muscle fibers in which deterioration and inflammation occur in a random fashion. Pathological changes also occur in the heart, particularly in myotonic dystrophy. Gradual disruption of myocardial fibers, alterations in muscular mitochondria and continued degeneration of other organelles within the muscle cells progress, resulting in gradual muscular weakness. Usually the diagnosis is made in childhood. Some of these children are merely considered clumsy, while others receive specialized orthopedic care because of difficulties in walking. Oftentimes the diagnosis is more obvious to those health professionals who are well-versed in the diagnosis of MD.

Unfortunately, there is no specific remedy for muscular dystrophy. Physical medicine and rehabilitation remain the best treatments of choice. Various exercises, splints, braces and corrective orthopedic appliances are engaged to offer those with MD a better quality of life. Since Coenzyme Q10 was shown to improve energy production in the heart's muscle cells, early pioneers questioned whether or not it might also strengthen the construction of skeletal muscle. The late Karl Folkers performed two double-blind studies in patients with progressive muscular dystrophy to explore the possibilities.

Folkers and colleagues conducted a limited three-month double-blind crossover trial to evaluate the oral administration of Coenzyme Q10 in 12 patients with progressive muscular dystrophy and neurogenic atrophies that included Charcot-Marie tooth disease and Welander disease. Patients ranged from 7 to 69 years of age. The Coenzyme Q10 whole blood levels were low, ranging from 0.5 to 0.84 ug/ml. In this limited three-month trial, the authors found that improved physical well-being was observed in four of eight treated patients. None of the control patients showed any improvement. Since the results revealed a significant increase in blood Coenzyme Q10 levels with Coenzyme Q10 supplementation, the authors concluded that Coenzyme Q10 represented a known substance that offered a safe and improved quality of life for these patients.[1]

Folkers then followed up this study a decade later with a second double-blind trial to evaluate 15 patients having the same categories of disease. Since cardiac disease is frequently seen in these muscular diseases, Folkers felt that the improved physical performance was related to the positive impact Coenzyme Q10 had on the entire muscular structure, including the heart. Although Dr. Folkers felt the 100 mg dosage was low, it was effective and safe. He concluded that any patient suffering from muscular dystrophy should be treated with CoQ10 indefinitely.[2]

MITOCHONDRIAL ENCEPHALOPATHY

Another category of muscular degenerative, mitochondrial encephalopathy disorders characterized by distinct clinical and biochemical

abnormalities includes the mitochondrial diseases that result from severe mitochondrial dysfunction. These illnesses are usually progressive
and multisystem in nature, involving the central nervous system, muscles, eyes, liver and kidneys. Muscle biopsies frequently shows characteristic irregular, ragged, red fibers and abnormal levels of
mitochondrial enzymes. Most of these patients are asymptomatic in
their early years and present to a doctor during their young adult years
with progressive eye problems including muscle weakness and easy
fatigability. Multisystem dysfunction with progressive hearing loss,
retinal deterioration and peripheral neuropathy are also common.
Many of these patients are significantly disabled and die from cardiac
causes, stroke or progressive dementia. In the mitochondrial syndromes, the clinical course is often unpredictive, and appropriate treatments have yet to be well-established. Isolated case reports, however,
have shown that Coenzyme Q10 may enhance mitochondrial function
and improve exercise tolerance as well as quality of life for these individuals. What does a typical case of mitochondrial myopathy look like
and how does it present? The following is a typical case report which
was published in *Neurology* in 1992.[3]

A 24-year-old male had been suffering from exercise intolerance
since the age of 15. At age 17, he developed weakening of the eyelids
and paralysis of the eye muscles. On physical examination, he had loss
of muscle on the right side of the body with a limb-girdle weakness (a
weakness in the thighs and hip girdle). An MRI of the brain showed
mild cortical atrophy. A muscle biopsy demonstrated the ragged red
fibers associated with myopathic changes. After a diagnosis of a mitochondrial myopathy syndrome was made, the patient was treated with
CoQ10 at a dosage of 150 mg daily. There was no family history or similar disease in any of the patient's relatives.

Specific mitochondrial DNA mutations have been identified in
which the clinical expression of these syndromes occur in the pediatric
age group or even later on in life. It is important that the clinician be
able to recognize these syndromes so appropriate treatments, particularly with Coenzyme Q10, can be administered. In this case study as
well as in the case of an 18-year-old male without a positive family history of mitochondrial myopathy, also discussed in the same journal,
ten months of CoQ10 treatment resulted in clinical improvement as
well as better mitochondrial function. Both patients showed an improvement in exercise tolerance as well. It is postulated that the ad-

ministration of CoQ10 as an electron acceptor may be indicated because of its ability to transport electrons to the superoxide and hydrogen peroxide radicals. These free radicals are then converted into harmless water and oxygen molecules with the assistance of the natural antioxidant enzymes superoxide dismutase and catalase. For this group of patients, long-term CoQ10 therapy helped to improve mitochondrial function resulting in an improvement in quality of life.

In a recent study involving six patients with mitochondrial cytopathies, 150 mg of CoQ10 over a six-month period showed improvement in brain variables as well as muscle mitochondrial function.[4] The investigators concluded that the beneficial effect of CoQ10 in these patients is consistent with the improvement in oxidative phosphorylation as a result of the increased CoQ10 concentration in the blood.

In another case study of mitochondrial encephalomyopathy, a 16-year-old boy with seizures, muscle weakness, mental retardation and progressive hearing loss was administered high dose CoQ10 therapy. After the additional administration of idebenone (an experimental drug used in Alzheimer's disease) was added to the CoQ10 protocol, the progression of clinical abnormalities was halted for 16 months.[5] If one reviews the literature on this disease and goes over individual case reports, it is apparent that CoQ10 does increase well-being and decrease muscular fatigability. In many of these patients, however, eye signs (ophthalmoplegia) were less likely to improve.

In another case study, a MELAS syndrome was reported after the individual had received long-term simvastatin therapy.[6] In this case a 63-year-old woman who had an unremarkable family history for MELAS had been treated with simvastatin for her hypercholesterolemia at a dose of 20 mg a day for eight months. When she was subsequently admitted to a hospital with generalized muscle weakness, her laboratory evaluation demonstration extreme elevations of muscle enzymes in the blood associated with signs of acute muscle inflammation. Neurological evaluation revealed drooping of the eyelids and vision problems. Following the withdrawal of simvastatin, there was an improvement in the blood levels of muscle breakdown products; however, the woman was left with some intellectual deficit and difficulty speaking. Fortunately, the eye problems resolved within four months. A muscle biopsy three months after admission showed the ragged red fibers characteristic of the MELAS syndrome. Her muscle CoQ10 concentration was low and, after three months treatment with oral CoQ10, 250 mg a day, subsequent muscle biopsies showed no ragged red fibers and the CoQ10 concentration had returned to normal range.

This case report is noteworthy because it is quite conceivable that this form of cholesterol-lowering therapy caused the MELAS syndrome to be expressed. If CoQ10 levels drop as a result of using statin-like drugs, could a mitochondrial disorder become manifest as seen in this case study? It is important for physicians to use statin drugs with caution, especially in patients who are prone to congestive heart failure and lower CoQ10 levels may result in the worsening of their cardiac function. The same situation may occur in an unrecognized or clinically silent mitochondrial disorder.

Although a broad discussion regarding mitochondrial encephalomyopathy is beyond the scope of this book, it is important to be aware of these syndromes, especially since treatment with Coenzyme Q10 has provided patients with a better quality of life. It is also interesting to note that many of these patients with defective mitochondria have characteristics of premature aging as well.

18

Side Effects, Contraindications, Drug Interactions

I have been prescribing Coenzyme Q10 for over a decade and have yet to see any significant adverse reactions, despite the fact that many of my patients take hundreds of milligrams daily. Occasionally, however, some patients have had to discontinue the nutrient because they reported they had too much energy. After taking Q10, they experienced a caffeine-like effect—the kind of energy surge you might feel after a cup of coffee. At times, even 10 mg caused a jittery effect in some patients, so they had to discontinue it. For these individuals, I recommend they get Q10 from food sources such as salmon, mackerel or sardines.

Another helpful tip: Q10 should not be taken prior to bedtime. Many of my patients, as well as those in clinical studies, have had difficulty falling asleep when Coenzyme Q10 was taken in the evening. In fact, in one of our research projects some of the patients in the experimental group asked to discontinue Q10. They reported that they could not tolerate the nutrient because of difficulty with sleeping and a feeling of too much energy.

Other unpleasant reactions that patients have told me about when taking Coenzyme Q10 include palpitations, diarrhea, appetite loss and mild nausea. Frequently these symptoms will disappear if Coenzyme Q10 is taken after meals, or if the dose is reduced. Rarely have I had to take patients off Coenzyme Q10 altogether because of these side effects.

The literature has also reported on the minimal side effect profiles and the safety of Coenzyme Q10 over long-term usage in 5,000 patients.

Adverse Events Reported for CoQ10 in 5,000 Patients[1]

Symptom	% of Patients
Epigastric discomfort	0.39
Decreased appetite	0.23
Nausea	0.16
Diarrhea	0.12
Elevated LDH	rare
Elevated SGOT	rare

In one small but interesting study of ten patients with Huntington's Chorea receiving 600–1200 mg of CoQ10 daily, adverse effects were assessed by telephone interview every month by the investigators. Although four subjects reported headache, heartburn, fatigue and increased involuntary movements, the tolerability of extremely high doses of Coenzyme Q10 show that it is a safe nutrient to be used in long-term clinical studies to slow the progression of Huntington's disease.[2] Since all the subjects completed the study, it would appear that these side effects were mild and, since a placebo group was not included, we do not know whether these mild side effects were due to CoQ10, Huntington's disease or even some other factors. When I look at my long clinical experience as well as reviewing the literature, the safety of Coenzyme Q10 is unquestioned.

CONTRAINDICATIONS

Although I don't know of any absolute contraindications, I would not recommend the routine use of Coenzyme Q10 for healthy pregnant women, nursing mothers, the newborn or even very young children. There is not yet enough data on the use of Coenzyme Q10 in these populations. However, in one study of 483 pregnant women, 49 patients presenting with spontaneous abortion had a tendency toward low CoQ10 blood levels.[3] The authors suggested further study to see if CoQ10 blood levels could be used as a marker to follow high-risk pregnancies. In a previous study, similar investigators reported low

Coenzyme Q10 levels in complicated pregnancy, especially in cases of spontaneous abortion before twelve weeks.[4] These findings were again demonstrated in the present study, suggesting a significant relationship between spontaneous abortion, threatened abortion and low levels of plasma CoQ10. When considering CoQ10 usage in pregnancy, the physician must obviously follow the patient's progress carefully.

There are also other situations when there may be specific indications for CoQ10 therapy, such as when heart failure occurs in a pregnant woman or when congestive heart failure occurs in a young child. In these situations, the physician should monitor the patient's progress when using Coenzyme Q10.

DRUG INTERACTIONS

In all my years of experience with Coenzyme Q10, I have only seen a few major drug interactions. This is particularly remarkable because I use Coenzyme Q10 in combination with many cardiac drugs. I have already discussed the Q10-depleting effects of some cholesterol-lowering drugs, i.e., the statins. I would also like to review some other drug interactions that have been reported.

For example, beta blockers have been shown to inhibit CoQ10-dependent enzymes. I have often wondered why a patient with congestive heart failure who was taking beta blockers occasionally worsened. Was it due to Coenzyme Q10 depletion? Perhaps so. Although I frequently prescribe Coenzyme Q10 and beta blockers for my patients, I am mindful about the Q10-depleting effects of these drugs.[5] On the plus side, Coenzyme Q10 has been known to reduce the drug-induced fatigue frequently experienced by people taking beta blockers.[6] Over the years, I have used Coenzyme Q10 in conjunction with beta blockers with much success, especially for the treatment of high blood pressure, arrhythmia and angina. The combination of CoQ10 and beta blockers works quite well in these situations.

Another group of drugs known to inhibit CoQ10-dependent enzymes is a class of psychotropic drugs including phenothiazine and tricyclic antidepressants.[7] I have often seen patients in my practice with arrhythmia, congestive heart failure and cardiomyopathy who have been taking these drugs over a long period of time. I have also often wondered why an occasional patient develops cardiomyopathy and congestive heart failure on these drugs. Perhaps it is CoQ10 inhibition with impaired oxidative phosphorylation and ATP production, all of which may inhibit energy that supports myocardial contractility.

The problem is that while many patients need to take these drugs in order to function in society, the concern about the cardiac effects of these drugs is warranted. Clinical studies have shown that Coenzyme Q10 supplementation has improved the EKGs in patients taking psychoactive drugs.[8] When I see patients in my practice who must take these medications but are having some cardiovascular side effects, I prescribe Coenzyme Q10 to help offset the possibility of these adverse effects.

Another area of potential concern is the use of Coenzyme Q10 in patients taking Coumadin, a commonly prescribed blood thinner. In 1994, a physician's letter to the editor in the *Lancet* reported three cases in which the effect of Coumadin was reduced by the simultaneous use of Coenzyme Q10.[9] The reporting physician attributed this interaction to CoQ10, which he suggested had a vitamin K–like effect. Yet, I have had patients on Coumadin who ate foods high in vitamin K (like broccoli or spinach) the night before their bloodwork, and they too counteracted their Coumadin and dipped down their protimes.

Coumadin (warfarin) is taken to increase the protime, the time it takes several clotting factors to form a clot. Coumadin is commonly used to prevent blood clotting in atrial fibrillation, valvular problems and other medical problems where clot formation is a concern. But frequently protimes will change and may be related to diet, temperature changes and many other drugs. That's why those on Coumadin are given dietary restrictions and should tell their physician if they are on any other over-the-counter medications.

Since the physician reported three cases in which Coumadin was affected by CoQ10 in his letter to the *Lancet* editor, it may be that CoQ10 does slow protime and so could have a blunting effect on Coumadin therapy. This possibility should raise interest in performing a double-blind study to scientifically determine the effect of CoQ10 on protimes, controlling for all the other variables I mentioned.

New research also indicates that Q10 may also reduce platelet stickiness, which could help prevent clot formation, a desirable effect for prevention of thrombo episodes. I carefully monitor protimes in my patients on Coumadin. If I feel that they need CoQ10 therapy as well, I know that I can always titrate the dose of each to keep both the symptoms and the protimes at therapeutic levels. However, I have never seen any problems in those patients who do take both CoQ10 and Coumadin, under my supervision.

Conclusion:
The Future of CoQ10

CoQ10 is a vital compound that is the very spark that keeps our complex human biochemical processes going. Unfortunately, many physicians do not recommend its use in clinical medicine. Although the rationale for CoQ10 in the treatment of a wide variety of diseases has been published in a number of controlled and uncontrolled studies, it continues to be underutilized by most American physicians. This, indeed, is unfortunate especially since Coenzyme Q10 may not only improve quality of life, but is actually essential for life to exist. Without widespread physician support, its potential as a literal lifesaver may never be fully realized for those who need it the most. Hopefully, if more double-blind research continues to show an improvement in measurable clinical response, more physicians will become comfortable in recommending CoQ10 to their patients.

We also must keep in mind that although CoQ10 has shown dramatic lifesaving value in selected patients, it is not a magic bullet that will guarantee a cure or even a better quality of life for all people. Although approximately 90 percent of patients will respond to CoQ10, 10 percent of patients do not improve despite excellent blood levels. Other related nutritional deficiencies must then be considered. Remember, in order for CoQ10 to recognize its full potential, an adequate supply of nutrients, enzymes, B vitamins, minerals and cofactors are necessary. The biosynthesis of CoQ10 is a complex 17-step process requiring seven vitamins and several trace elements; a suboptimal nutrient intake could impair the formation and action of the compound.

This is why a healthy diet is a must whenever we incorporate any targeted nutritional support, like CoQ10, into our daily regimen. But what is a healthy diet? Is low fat better than no fat? Is a high carbohydrate diet the answer? This has been the subject of much controversy.

THE BEST DIET

Over the years, I have contemplated the merits of various dietary regimes, and have come to the conclusion that the best overall diet in disease prevention is the Mediterranean Diet.

The Mediterranean Diet not only emphasizes fish, an excellent source of CoQ10, but it also contains all the raw materials necessary to synthesize CoQ10 in the body. In addition, the Mediterranean Diet includes substantial key phytonutrients and various vitamins, minerals, carotenoids, flavonoids, polyphenols and Omega-3 essential fatty acids that are so essential to our well being, especially our cardiac health.

THE BENEFITS OF THE MEDITERRANEAN DIET

1. Fish and shellfish are excellent sources of CoQ10.
2. Contains an abundance of beneficial essential fatty acids, the omega-3 oils that reduce clotting and inflammation.
3. Offers a cornucopia of fresh fruits and fresh vegetables with carotenoids, flavonoids, vitamins, polyphenols—heart-healthy phytonutrients.
4. Low in dairy and excessive quantities of meat, thus less arachidonic acid.
5. Rich in root vegetables such as garlic/onions, terrific heart healers.
6. Antioxidant-rich in vitamin C, vitamin E, magnesium, zinc and L-glutathione.
7. High in legumes such as lentils and chickpeas, which lower insulin levels.
8. Low in saturated fat, high in fiber, creating less insulin resistance.

9. High in olive oil, which is far healthier than margarine which contains transfatty acids.
10. May include red wine, a rich source of quercetin which prevents the deposit of arterial plaque.

The Lyon Heart Diet Study which followed 605 patients concluded that those on a Mediterranean-style diet deriving approximately 35 percent of their calories from healthy fats had substantial cardiac protection with 76 percent fewer cardiac events including subsequent heart attacks than those who followed their doctors' dietary advice or the typical American Heart Association Diet.[2,3]

The Mediterranean Diet is also the most balanced way of eating carbohydrates, healthy fats and proteins. By limiting carbohydrate intake to approximately 50 percent of calories, using healthy fats such as those found in fish, seafood, nuts, tofu and olive oil along with generous helpings of protein, insulin resistance, a major health hazard affecting our population today, can be prevented.

I believe the most cardiac-protective dietary balance is approximately 50 percent carbohydrates, 30 percent healthy fats and 20 percent protein. Using fewer processed carbohydrates and sugars, and more complex carbohydrates (chickpeas, lentils and broccoli, for example) will drop insulin levels, sparing our vascular system from insulin excess, a major cause of heart disease. Diet-induced insulin resistance may be expressed over time as weight gain, low HDL cholesterol and high serum triglycerides, major risk factors for coronary heart disease.

Thus, I believe the trendy zero-fat or very low-fat diets are hazardous to our health. For a more detailed review of the health benefits of the Mediterranean Diet, see my recent book, *Optimum Health*. For my modified Mediterranean Diet Meal Plan, see the Appendix.

IS COQ10 TOO GOOD TO BE TRUE?

My clinical experience of seeing patients on a day-to-day basis has taught me some of the most important aspects of healing. My patients have been my best teachers. Their multifaceted needs have been the signposts on my road to professional development. What they needed, I studied. It's an exciting and ongoing process with no end in sight, and I'm continuously overwhelmed by how much I still don't know. One thing that I have witnessed over the years is the multifaceted healing capabilities of Coenzyme Q10. But when a substance like Coenzyme Q10 is touted for so many pathological ailments, it sounds just too good to be true. This probably raises much skepticism, and rightly so. But despite the excessive hype, double-blind research has demonstrated that CoQ10 shows real promise, especially in heart health and some of the other degenerative diseases discussed in this book. These well-conducted studies with substantial findings will hopefully attract researchers to study CoQ10 in greater detail.

Although magic bullets, quick-fixes and panaceas do not really exist when we become ill, Coenzyme Q10 is a proven nutrient with prophylactic and therapeutic value. When taken in combination with a healthy diet and proper supplementation, CoQ10 has a greater chance for achieving maximum potential. Remember that the "pulsation" of cells is the most basic and essential function of life. CoQ10's magic is in its ability to produce cellular energy, stabilize membranes and administer antioxidant protection. Although CoQ10's natural healing properties are common in many foods, supplementation is definitely required for medicinal purposes. When it comes to natural healing, I always reflect on the words of Thomas Alva Edison who said, more than a century ago,

> The doctor of the future will give no medicine, but will interest his patients in the care of the human frame, in diet, and in the cause and prevention of disease.

I believe that the Coenzyme Q10 phenomenon is a testimony to Edison's insightful remark.

The Sinatra Modified Mediterranean Diet Seven–Day Meal Plan*

Day One

Breakfast

    ½ whole wheat English muffin or
    1 slice of whole wheat bread
    Phytoestrogen Shake (recipe on page 141)
    ¹/₃ melon

Lunch

    1 4 oz. veggie burger served with romaine lettuce, sliced
      tomato & onion
    2 slices whole wheat bread
    1 cup coleslaw mixed with 1 T. plain nonfat yogurt and 6
      chopped walnuts
    1 apple

Dinner

    6 oz. salmon steak
    1 cup couscous
    1 cup broccoli steamed with
      2 T. sesame seeds and a dash of
      fresh squeezed lemon

*Reprinted from Stephen Sinatra's *HeartSense*, with permission from Phillips Publishing, Inc.

Sliced tomato salad with chopped onion, garlic and
1 tsp. olive oil or flax oil with balsamic vinegar

Broil steak sprinkled with ½ lemon for 5 minutes. Use other lemon half on the broccoli. Chop 1 small onion and 1 clove garlic for the sliced tomato and dress with oil and vinegar to taste.

Day Two

Breakfast

1 cup oatmeal
½ cup berries of choice
1 cup soy milk (½ cup in oatmeal—the other ½ cup as a
beverage)

Lunch

6 oz. sardines (or mackerel) in a sandwich (or substitute
veggie burger)
topped with onion slices & 1 T. low-fat mayo
2 toasted slices of whole grain bread
2 cups tossed green side salad with 1 T. flax or
olive oil mixed with fresh lemon juice or balsamic vinegar to
taste
2 plums

Dinner

Stir-fried vegetables with 8 oz. chopped tofu
3 cloves garlic, chopped
1 T. olive oil
2 T. fresh Parmesan cheese
1½ cups cooked brown rice with chopped onion

In a wok or large frying pan, steam 3 cloves chopped fresh garlic with chopped vegetables (1 small bunch broccoli, 12 mushrooms, 2 medium zucchini, 2 medium summer squash, peppers, etc.) steamed in 3–4 oz. water. Drizzle oil and cheese over veggies when tender. Serve over brown rice.

Day Three

Breakfast

> Buckwheat pancakes (recipe on page 144)
> ½ cup chopped walnuts or almonds for topping
> 2 T. real maple syrup

Lunch

> ¾ cup chickpea hummus spread with
>   sliced tomato, leafy green lettuce and
>   ½ sliced avocado on whole wheat pita bread
> 1 cup cooked White Bean Salad with olive oil (see recipe on
>   page 146)
> 6 walnuts, chopped
> 1 peach

Dinner

> ½ baked boned/skinless chicken breast
> 2 T. mango chutney
> 1 cup new potatoes with
>   2 cloves chopped garlic, 1 small chopped onion
>   and 1 tsp. olive oil
> 6–8 asparagus spears steamed and sprinkled with fresh
>   lemon juice and a pinch of garlic salt

Bake chicken spread with chutney for 20 minutes at 400°F. Combine chopped potatoes with garlic, onions and oil and bake for 25 minutes at the same temperature.

Day Four

Breakfast

> Blueberry Bran muffin (recipe on page 142)
> Phytoestrogen Shake (recipe on page 141)
> 1–2 kiwis, peeled and sliced

Lunch

    1 cup low-fat cottage cheese served with
      ½ sliced cucumber, ½ sliced avocado with
    1 T. flax or olive oil mixed with 1 tsp. lemon juice
    ½ baked acorn or butternut squash
    1 peach

Dinner

    8 oz. shrimp sautéed with 2 chopped garlic cloves
    1 chopped small onion and 1 T. olive oil served over 1 cup
      cooked brown rice
    1½ cups spinach salad with one chopped garlic clove, 4 raw
      cauliflower florets and 4 sliced strawberries served with
      lemon-honey dressing (recipe on page 141)

Day Five

Breakfast

    2-egg omelet (use organic eggs or those from hens fed
      flaxseed)
    1 bran muffin (recipe on page 142) with fruit spread (try a
      purée of your favorite fruit)
    ½ grapefruit

Lunch

    ½ can white tuna (packed in water) drained and mixed with
    1 cup red kidney beans and 1 tsp. balsamic vinegar
    1 cup cooked tabouli with chopped tomato, mint and
      1 tsp. olive oil
    3–4 fresh whole apricots

Dinner

    Pasta Primavera (see recipe on page 145)
    1½ cups Jerusalem artichoke or whole wheat linguine pasta
    Small Caesar salad with two ground anchovies, mixed with
      1 T. olive oil, 2 T. Parmesan cheese and fresh-squeezed
      lemon juice

Day Six

Breakfast

> Wheat, bran, spelt or kamut dry cereal
>   (Arrowhead Mills/Nature's Path brands in your health
>   food store)
> 1½ cups soy milk (½ on cereal and ½ as a beverage)
> ½ cup berries or 1 banana sliced

Lunch

> Antiguan Black Bean Soup (recipe on page 143)
> 2 slices multi-grain bread
> 1 shredded carrot salad with walnuts and
>   1 T. low-fat yogurt
> Cherries

Dinner

> Grilled Mediterranean Halibut (recipe on page 147)
> 1½ cups Waldorf salad with romaine lettuce, pear slices,
>   walnuts, lemon-honey dressing (recipe on page 141)
> 6–8 cauliflower florets, steamed

Day Seven

Breakfast

> 1 cup oatmeal mixed with 3 T. low-fat or fat-free cottage
>   cheese
> ½ cup of berries of your choice
> 1 cup soy milk (divided as in other breakfasts)

Lunch

> 1 large portabello mushroom cap, sliced and sauteed in lite
>   teriyaki sauce with
> 2 oz. chevre (goat's cheese or blue cheese)
> Sliced tomato and onion
> 2 slices whole grain bread or bun
> Green salad with 1 chopped clove garlic
> 1 T. olive/flax oil and fresh lemon juice
> 1 pear

Dinner

> Lentil stew (recipe on page 148) served over 1 cup cooked
> brown rice
> 6–8 asparagus spears, steamed (when cooked add
> 1 tsp. olive oil and a pinch of garlic salt)
> 2–3 cups raw, baby spinach salad topped with
> ¼ cup sliced strawberries, ¼ cup blueberries,
> 2 T. chopped pecans and walnuts with a raspberry
> vinaigrette dressing (includes 1 T. olive oil.)

Mediterranean Recipes

Phytoestrogen Shake

Flaxseed is considered one of the world's richest sources of omega-3s.

Grind 2 T. of organic flaxseed in a clean coffee mill. Add it to 8–10 oz. chilled soy milk plus $^{1}/_{2}$ banana, 4 strawberries or 2 T. blueberries. Whip it up in your blender.

Lemon–Honey Dressing

Ingredients

Juice of one large lemon
2 T. honey
2 T. olive oil
$^{1}/_{2}$ tsp. dried basil
Freshly ground pepper to taste

Blueberry Bran Muffins

2 cups bran cereal
1 cup skim milk
1 T. grapeseed oil
2 egg whites
1 T. honey
$^1/_3$ cup molasses
$1^1/_2$ cups whole wheat flour or Soy Quik flour
$^1/_2$ tsp. sea salt
1 cup blueberries

Mix bran cereal and milk and let stand 5 minutes. Add oil, egg whites, honey and molasses. Add flour, salt and blueberries. Stir until just mixed. Bake in a muffin tin at 400 degrees for 15 minutes.

Antiguan Black Bean Soup

2 T. olive oil
$^1/_2$ green pepper, chopped
1 onion, chopped
$^1/_2$ clove garlic, minced
$^1/_2$ lb. dried black beans, cooked according to package directions, or substitute 2 one-pound cans of drained black beans
2 quarts water
Freshly ground pepper
2 T. red wine vinegar
1 bay leaf
1 cup short-grain brown rice, cooked
Fresh parsley, chopped

In a large saucepan, combine olive oil, green pepper, onion (reserve some raw onion as a topping) and garlic. Sauté until tender. Add precooked or canned black beans, pepper, vinegar and bay leaf. Add water and then simmer for 30 to 40 minutes. Remove bay leaf before serving. Top with raw onion and brown rice. Garnish with parsley.

Buckwheat Pancakes with Blueberries

1 cup buckwheat flour
1 cup other whole grain flour
2 cups soy milk or water
2 eggs
1 T. grapeseed oil
1 T. honey
$1/3$ cup fresh unsweetened blueberries

Stir dry ingredients together. Add soy milk, eggs, oil and honey and mix briefly. Add blueberries and stir gently. Cook on hot lightly oiled griddle.

Pasta Primavera

2 cups fresh broccoli florets
1 cup fresh asparagus spears, chopped
1 cup sun-dried tomatoes (not oil-packed)
2 small zucchini, chopped
2–3 cloves garlic, chopped
1 small onion, chopped
1 cup grated carrot
1 cup fresh, chopped parsley
2 T. fresh Parmesan cheese
1 T. olive oil
2 cups Jerusalem artichoke or whole wheat linguine or angel
   hair pasta

Steam the broccoli and asparagus for 2–3 minutes in a vegetable steamer. In a large skillet, gently sauté the chopped onion and garlic before adding remaining vegetables. (You may add 3–4 T. water while sautéing, if necessary.) Sauté vegetables and sun-dried tomatoes for 5 minutes. Add partially cooked broccoli and asparagus, and sauté for another minute.

Cook the pasta according to directions. After draining, mix with sautéed vegetables and gently toss with Parmesan cheese and chopped parsley. Serves 3–4, so you may eat any leftovers warm or cold the next day.

White Bean Salad

½ lb. dry white beans (washed and soaked overnight) or sub-
    stitute 2 cans cooked white beans, drained
3½ cups water
1 medium onion and 2 garlic cloves, chopped
1 medium red or Vidalia onion, chopped finely
1 bunch fresh parsley, chopped
1 yellow or red pepper, chopped
½ tsp. dried mustard
1 minced garlic clove
1 T. flax or olive oil
Lemon juice and balsamic vinegar to taste

Drain the beans, add water and place in a pot with coarsely chopped onion and 2 garlic cloves. After bringing to a boil, simmer for 1½ hours or until tender. Drain and reserve ¼ cup cooking liquid.

Mix pepper, minced garlic, oil, mustard, lemon juice and vinegar together with reserved cooking liquid. Add to warm beans and toss with fresh parsley. (If you are in a hurry, use canned beans and flavor with extra lemon juice to taste.) Serves 3–4.

Grilled Halibut Mediterranean Style with Lemon–Basil Vinaigrette

4 4–6 oz. halibut steaks, ¾ inch thick
1 lemon
½ tsp. grated lemon peel
2 T. olive oil
3 garlic cloves, crushed
3 T. fresh basil or 3 tsp. dried
2 tsp. drained capers
Sea salt and pepper to taste

Squeeze lemon. Whisk lemon juice, olive oil, garlic and lemon peel in a small bowl to blend. Stir in 2 T. fresh basil and the capers. Season vinaigrette to taste with salt and pepper.

Preheat boiler to medium-high heat. Season halibut steaks with salt and pepper. Brush fish with 1 T. vinaigrette. Grill or broil halibut steaks until just cooked through, about 4 minutes per side. Transfer fish to plates. Re-whisk remaining vinaigrette; pour over fish. Garnish fish with remaining basil and serve. Serves 4.

Lentil Stew

1 cup uncooked red or green lentils
4 cups water
1 medium onion, chopped
1 stalk celery, chopped
2 leeks (white part only), sliced
1 medium zucchini, chopped
1 sweet potato or yam, chopped
1 low-sodium vegetable broth seasoning cube
2 garlic cloves, chopped
1 cup fresh parsley, chopped
1 T. balsamic vinegar

Bring lentils to a boil and simmer until tender. Generally, green lentils take twice the time as red so allow 45 minutes for green and about 20 minutes for red lentils.

In a skillet or wok, sauté chopped onion and garlic for 1 minute. Add chopped sweet potato (or yam) and sauté for 5 minutes. Add ¼ cup of water, vegetable boullion and remaining vegetables. Cover and steam for 5 minutes.

When vegetables are tender, mix in lentils, toss with chopped parsley and vinegar and serve. Serves 3–4.

HEART HEALTHY EXTRAS

This seven-day meal plan has 1700 calories per day. Snacks, beverages and desserts following dinner are at your discretion. But remember, try not to let more than four hours go by without at least a small, healthy snack.

Snacks: Fresh fruits such as apples, peaches, plums, cherries, strawberries, kiwi and rhubarb are in the complex carbohydrate category. Raw vegetables such as broccoli, cauliflower, celery or a handful of walnuts, pumpkin seeds or almonds help to stop carbo cravings.

Beverages: Try to drink 8 glasses of water or herbal teas per day. If you must drink fruit juice you may have 4 oz. of juice diluted with 2 oz. of water per day. You may also drink 4 oz. of red wine each day.

Desserts: Again, you may eat the fruits listed as snacks. For example, strawberries are only 50 calories per cup and are high in phytonutrients, antioxidants and fiber. For a special treat, try dipping a banana in orange juice and 1 T. of finely chopped walnuts.

Notes

Introduction

1. Tanaka, J., et al., Coenzyme Q10: The prophylactic effect of low cardiac output following cardiac valve replacement. *Ann Thorac Surg*, 1982; 33:145–51.
2. Carper J., *Miracle Cures*, New York: HarperCollins Publishing, Inc., 1997.

Chapter 1: CoQ10: A Miracle in Our Midst

1. Frishman, W. H., et al., Innovative pharmacologic approaches for the treatment of myocardial ischemia. In: Frishman, W. H., Sonnenblick, E. H., eds., *Cardiovascular Pharmaotherapeutics*. New York; McGraw-Hill 1997: 846–850.

Chapter 2: History of CoQ10

1. Crane, F. L., et al., Isolation of a quinone from beef heart mitochondria. *Biochimica et Biophys Acta*, 1957; 25:220–221.
2. Littarru, G. P., *Energy and Defense*. Rome, 1995; 14–24.
3. Littarru, G. P., Ho, L., and Folkers, K., Deficiency of Coenzyme Q10 in human heart disease. Part I and II. *Internat. J Vit Nutr Res*, 1972; 42(2):291:42(3)413.
4. Mitchell, P., Possible molecular mechanisms of the protonmotive function of cytochrome systems. *J Theoret Biol*, 1976; 62:327–367.
5. Yamamura, Y. A survey of the therapeutic uses of Coenzyme Q. In: Tenaz, G. (ed.): *Coenzyme Q*. John Wiley & Sons Ltd. New York, 492–493. 1985.
6. Langsjoen, P. H., Vadhanavikit, S. and Folkers, K., Response of patients in classes III and IV of cardiomyopathy to therapy in a blind and crossover trial with Coenzyme Q10. *Proc Natl Acad of Sci*, 1985; 82:4240–4244.
7. Ernster, L., and Forsmark, P., Ubiquinol: an endogenous antioxidant in aerobic organisms. Seventh International Symposium on Biomedical and

Clinical Aspects of Coenzyme Q. Folkers, K., et al. (eds.) *The Clin Inves*, 1993; Suppl. 71(8):S60–S65.

8. Hashiba, K., et al., *Heart* 1972; 4:1579–1589 (in Japanese).

9. Iwabuchi, T., et al., *Jpn J Clin Exp Med*, 1972; 49, 2604–08 (in Japanese).

10. Imajuki, S., et al., *Jpn J Pediatr*, 1981; 44:1183–1186 (in Japanese).

11. Hiasa, Y., et al., Effects of coenzyme Q10 on exercise tolerance in patients with stable angina pectoris. In: Folkers, K., Yamamura, Y., (eds.) *Biomedical and Clinical Aspects of Coenzyme Q*, Elsevier, Amsterdam, 1981; 3:291–301.

12. Kamikawa, T., et al., Effects of coenzyme Q10 on exercise tolerance in chronic stable angina pectoris. *Am J Cardiol*, 1985; 56:247–251.

13. Langsjoen, P. H., et al., Response of patients in classes III and IV of cardiomyopathy to therapy in a blind and crossover trial with coenzyme Q10. *Proc Natl Acad of Sci*, 1985; 82:4240–4244.

14. Judy, W. V., et al., Double blind-double crossover study of coenzyme Q10 in heart failure. In: Folkers, K., Yamamura, Y. (eds.) *Biomedical and Clinical Aspects of Coenzyme Q*, Elsevier, Amsterdam 1986; 5:315–323.

15. Schneeberger, W., et al., A clinical double-blind and crossover trial with coenzyme Q10 on patients with cardiac disease. In: Folkers, K., Yamamura, Y., (eds.) *Biomedical and Clinical Aspects of Coenzyme Q10*, Elsevier, Amsterdam, 1986; 5:325–333.

16. Permanetter, B., et al., Lack of effectiveness of coenzyme Q10 (ubiquinone) in long-term treatment of dilated cardiomyopathy. Original Title: Fehlende Wirksamkeit von Coenzyme Q10 (Ubichinon) bei der Langzeitbehandlung der dilataiven Kardiomyopathie. *Z Kardiol*, 1989; 78(6):360–5 (in German).

17. Rossi, E., et al., Coenzyme Q10 in ischaemic cardiopathy. In: Folkers, K., Yamagami, T., and Littarru, G. P. (eds.). *Biomedical and Clinical Aspects of Coenzyme Q*, Elsevier, Amsterdam. 1991; 6:321–326.

18. Schardt, F., et al., Effect of coenzyme Q10 on ischaemia-induced ST segment depression: A double blind, placebo-controlled crossover study. In: Folkers, K., Yamagami, T., and Littarru, G. P., (eds.) *Biomedical and Clinical Aspects of Coenzyme Q*. Elsevier, Amsterdam. 1991; 6:385–403.

19. Hoffman-Bang C., et al., Coenzyme Q10 as an adjunctive in treatment of congestive heart failure. *Am J of Cardiol*, 1992 Supplement 19 (3), 216A.

20. Permanetter, B., et al., Ubiquinone (coenzyme Q10) in the long-term treatment of idiopathic dilated cardiomyopathy. *Eur Heart J*, 1992; 11:1528–33.

21. Ghirlanda, G., et al., Evidence of plasma CoQ10-lowering effect by HMG-CoA reductase inhibitors: a double-blind, placebo-controlled study. *J Clin Pharm*, 1993; 33(3):226–9.

22. Morisco, C., Trimarco, B., Condorelli, M., Effect of coenzyme Q10 therapy in patients with congestive heart failure: A long-term multicenter ran-

domized study. In: Folkers, K., et al., (eds.) Seventh International Symposium on Biomedial and Clinical Aspects of Coenzyme Q. *The Clinical Investigator*, 1993; 71:S134–S136.

23. Kuklinski B., Weissenbacher E., Fahnrich A.: Coenzyme Q10 and antioxidants in acute myocardial infarction. *Mol Aspects Med*, 1994; 15 Suppl: s143–7.

24. Wilson, M. F., et al., Coenzyme Q10 therapy and exercise duration in stable angina. In: Folkers K., Littarru G. P., Yamagami T. (eds.) *Biomedical and Clinical Aspects of Coenzyme Q10*. 1991; 6:339–348.

25. Chello, M., et al., Protection by coenzyme Q10 from myocardial reperfusion injury during coronary artery bypass grafting. *Ann Thorac Surg*, 1994; 58(5):1427–32.

26. Taggart, D. P., et al., Effects of short-term supplementation with coenzyme Q10 on myocardial protection during cardiac operations. *Ann Thorac Surg*, 1996; 61(3):829–33.

27. *Biomedical and Clinical Aspects of Coenzyme Q*, (1977) Folkers, K., Yamamura, Y. (eds.) Elsevier, Amsterdam, pp 1–315.

28. *Biomedical and Clinical Aspects of Coenzyme Q*, vol. 2 (1980) Folkers, K., and Ito, Y. (eds.) Elsevier, Amsterdam, pp 1–456.

29. *Biomedical and Clinical Aspects of Coenzyme Q*, vol. 3 (1981) Folkers, K., Yamamura, Y. (eds.) Elsevier, Amsterdam, pp 1–414.

30. *Biomedical and Clinical Aspects of Coenzyme Q*, vol. 4 (1984) Folkers, K., Yamamura, Y. (eds.) Elsevier, Amsterdam, pp 1–432.

31. *Biomedical and Clinical Aspects of Coenzyme Q*, vol. 5 (1986) Folkers, K., Yamamura, Y. (eds.) Elsevier, Amsterdam, pp 1–410.

32. *Biomedical and Clinical Aspects of Coenzyme Q*, vol. 6 (1991) Folkers, K., Yamamura, Y., and Littarru, G. P. (eds.) Elsevier, Amsterdam, pp 1–555.

33. Seventh International Symposium on Biomedical and Clinical Aspects of Coenzyme Q. Folkers, K., et al., (eds.) *The Clin Inves*, 1993; 71(8):S51–S177.

34. Eighth International Symposium on Biomedical and Clinical Aspects of Coenzyme Q. Littarru, G. P., Battino, M., Folkers, K. (eds.) *The Molecular Aspects of Medicine*, 1994; 15:S1–S294.

35. Ninth International Symposium on Biomedical and Clinical Aspects of Coenzyme Q. Littarru, G. P., et al., (eds.) *Molecular Aspects of Medicine*, 1997; 18:S1–S309.

36 First International CoQ10 Association, Boston, 1998.

Chapter 3: Definition and Biochemistry of CoQ10

1. Littarru, G. P., *Energy and Defense*. Rome, 1995; 14–24.

2. Greenberg, S. and Frishman, W. H., Coenzyme Q10: A new drug for cardiovascular disease, *Clin Pharm*. 1990; 30:596–608.

3. Kidd, P. M., et al. Coenzyme Q10: Essential Energy Carrier and Antioxidant. *HK Biomedical Consultants*, 1988; 1–8.
4. Miquel, J. Theoretical and experimental support for an "oxygen radical-mitochondrial injury" hypothesis of cell aging. In: Johnson J. E., et al. (eds.) *Free Radicals, Aging, and Degenerative Diseases*. New York: Aland R. Liss; 1986; 51–55.
5. Smith, I. B., Ingerman, C. M. and Silver, M. J.: Malondialdehyde formation as an indicator of prostaglandin production by human platelets. *J Lab Clin Med*, 1976; 88:167–72.
6. Porter, N. A.: Prostaglandin endoperoxides. In: Pryor, W. A., ed, *Free Radicals in Biology*, vol 4, London, Academic Press; 1980; 261.
7. Stocker, R., Bowry, V. W., and Frei, B., Ubiquinol-10 protects human low-density lipoproteins more efficiently against lipid peroxidation than does *a*-tocopherol. *Proc Natl Acad Sci USA*, 1991; 88:1646–1650.
8. McGuire, J. J., et al., Succinate-ubiquinone reductase linked recycling of alphatocopherol in reconstituted systems and mitochondria: requirement for reduced ubiquinol. *Arch Biochem Biophys*, 1992; 292:47–53.
9. Serebruany, V. L., et al., Dietary Coenzyme Q10 supplementation alters platelet size and inhibits human bitronectin (CD51/CD61) receptor expression. *J Cardiovas Pharm*, 1997; 29:16–22.
10. Folkers, K., et al., The biomedical and clinical aspects of Coenzyme Q, *Clin Investig*, 1993; 71:S51–S178.

Chapter 4: How and When to Supplement with CoQ10

1. Kishi, T., et al., Serum levels of Coenzyme Q10 in patients receiving total parenteral nutrition and relationship of serum lipids. In: Folkers, K. and Yamamura, Y. (eds.) *Biomedical and Clinical Aspects of Coenzyme Q*, 1986; 5:119.
2. Kalen, A., Appelkvist, E. L., Dallner, G., Age-related changes in the lipid compositions of rat and human tissues. *Lipids*, 1989; 24:579–581.
3. Aryoma, O. I., Free Radicals and antioxidant strategies in sports. *J Nutr Biochem*, 1994; 5:370.
4. Ghirlanda, G., et al., Evidence of plasma CoQ10-lowering effect by HMG-CoA reductase inhibitors: A double-blind, placebo-controlled study. *J Clin Pharm*, 1993; 33(3):226–9.
5. Folkers, K., et al., Lovastatin decreases Coenzyme Q10 levels in humans. *Proc Natl Acad Sci*, 1990; 87:8931–8934.
6. Folkers, K., et al., Evidence for a deficiency of Coenzyme Q10 in human heart disease. *Int J Vitam Nutr Res*, 1970; 40:380–90.
7. Littarru, G. P., Ho, L. and Folkers, K., Deficiency of coenzyme Q10 in human heart disease. *Int J Vitam Nutr Res*, 1972; 42:291–305.

8. Mancini, A., et al., Evaluation of metabolic status in Amiodarone-induced thyroid disorders: Plasma Coenzyme Q10 determination, *J Endocrinol Invest*, 1989; 12:511–516.

9. Ernster, L., and Forsmark, P., Ubiquinol: An endogenous antioxidant in aerobic organisms, *Clin Investig*, 1993; 71:S62.

10. Hata T., Kunida H. and Oyama, Y., Antihypertensive effects of Coenzyme Q10 in essential hypertension, *Clin Endocrinol*, 1977; 25:1019–1022.

11. Maurer, I., Bernhard, A. and Zierz, S., Coenzyme Q10 and respiratory chain enzyme activities in hypertrophied human left ventricles with aortic valve stenosis, *Am J Cardiol*, 1990; 66:504–505.

12. Hanaki, Y., Coenzyme Q10 and coronary artery disease, *Clin Invest*, 1993; 71:S112–S115.

13. Yoshida, T., Maulik, G., Increased myocardial tolerance to ischemia-reperfusion injury by feeding pigs with Coenzyme Q10, *Ann NY Acad Sci*, 1996; 793:414–418.

14. Folkers, K., Perspectives from research on vitamins and hormones, *J Chem Educ*, 1984; 61:747–56.

15. Folkers, K., Vadhanavikit, S. and Mortensen, S. A., Biochemical rationale and myocardial tissue data on the effective therapy of cardiomyopathy with Coenzyme Q10, *Proc Natl Acad Sci USA*, 1985; 82(3):901–904.

16. Sinatra, S., CoQ10 formulation can influence bioavailability, *Nutrition Science News*, 1997; 2(2):88.

17. Chopra, R. et al., Relative bioavailability of Coenzyme Q10 formulations in human subjects. *International Journal for Vitamin and Mineral Research*, 1998.

18. Lansjoen, P. H., et al., Long-term efficacy and safety of Coenzyme Q10 therapy for idiopathic dilated cardiomyopathy, *Am J Cardiol*, 1990; 65:512–23.

19. Proceedings from the 9th International Conference on CoQ10, Ancona, 1996.

Chapter 5: Congestive Heart Failure and Cardiomyopathy

1. Folkers, K., Vadhanavikit, S., Mortensen, S. A., Biochemical rationale and myocardial tissue data on the effective therapy of cardiomyopathy with coenzyme Q10. *Proc Natl Acad Sci, USA*, 1985; 82(3):901–904.

2. Kamikawa T, et al., Effects of coenzyme Q10 on exercise tolerance in chronic stable angina pectoris, *Am J Cardiol*, 1985; 56:247–251.

3. Kuklinski, B., Weissenbacher, E., Fahnrich, A., Coenzyme Q10 and antioxidants in acute myocardial infarction, *Mol Aspects Med*, 1994; 15 Suppl: s143–7.

4. Hanaki, Y., Coenzyme Q10 and coronary artery disease, *Clin Invest*, 1993; 71:S112–S115.

5. Greenberg, S. M., Frishman, W. H., Coenzyme Q10: A new drug for cardiovascular disease, *Clin Pharm*, 1990; 30:596–608.

6. Hata, T., Kunida, H., Oyama, Y., Antihypertensive effects of Coenzyme Q10 in essential hypertension, *Clin Endocrinol*, 1977; 25:1019–1022.

7. Digiesi, V., Cantini, F., Brodbeck, B., Effect of Coenzyme Q10 on essential arterial hypertension, *Current Therapeutic Research*, 1990; 47:841–845.

8. Domac, N., Sawada, H., et al., Cardiomyopathy and other chronic toxic effects induced in rabbits by doxorubicin and possible prevention by Coenzyme Q10, *Cancer Treat Rep*, 1981; 65(1–2):79–91.

9. Takahashi, K., Mayumi, T., Kiski, T., Influence of Coenzyme Q10 on doxorubicin uptake and metabolism by mouse myocardial cells in culture, *Chem Pharm Bull*, 1988; 36:1514–1518.

10. Langsjoen, P. H., Vadhanavikit, S., Folkers, K., Response of patients in classes III and IV of cardiomyopathy to therapy in a blind and crossover trial with Coenzyme Q10. *Proc Natl Acad of Sci*, 1985; 82:4240–4244.

11. Hoffman-Bang, C., et al., Coenzyme Q10 as an adjunctive in treatment of congestive heart failure, *Am J of Cardiol*, 1992 Supplement 19(3), 216A.

12. Morisco, C., Trimarco, B., Condorelli, M., Effect of Coenzyme Q10 therapy in patients with congestive heart failure: A long-term multicenter randomized study. In: Folkers, K., et al., eds., Seventh International Symposium on Biomedial and Clinical Aspects of Coenzyme Q, *The Clinical Investigator*, 1993; 71:S134–S136.

13. Manzoli, U., Rossie, E., Littarru, G. P., et al., Coenzyme Q10 in dilated cardiomyopathy, *Int J Tissue React*, 1990; 12:173–8.

14. Judy, W. V., Folkers, K., Hall, J. H., Improved long-term survival in Coenzyme Q10 treated chronic heart failure patients compared to conventionally treated patients. In: *Biomedical and Clinical Aspects of Coenzyme Q*, vol 6, K. Folkers, G. P. Littarru and T. Yamagami, eds., 1991; 291–298.

15. Langsjoen, P. H., Folkers, K., Isolated diastolic dysfunction of the myocardium and its response to CoQ10 treatment, *Clin Invest*, 1993; 71:S140–S144.

16. Pogessi, L., et al., Effect of Coenzyme Q10 on left ventricular function in patients with dilated cardiomyopathy, *Current Therapy and Research*, 1991; 49:878–886.

17. Baggio, E., et al., Italian multicenter study on safety and efficacy of Coenzyme Q10, *The Molecular Aspects of Medicine*, 1994; 15:S287–S294.

18. Folkers, K., Littaru, G. P., Ho, L., et al., Evidence for a deficiency of Coenzyme Q10 in human heart disease, *Int J Vitam Nutr Res*, 1970; 40:380–90.

19. Littarru, G. P., Ho, L., Folkers, K., et al., Deficiency of Coenzyme Q10 in human heart disease I, *Int J Vitam Nutr Res*, 1972; 42:291–305.

20. Folkers, K., Perspectives from research on vitamins and hormones, *J Chem Educ*, 1984; 61:747–56.

21. Langsjoen, P. H., Langsjoen, P., Folkers, K., et al., Long-term efficacy and safety of Coenzyme Q10 therapy for idiopathic dilated cardiomyopathy, *Am J Cardiol*, 1990; 65:512–23.

22. Folkers, K., Langsjoen, P., Langsjoen, P. H., Therapy with Coenzyme Q10 of patients in heart failure who are eligible or ineligible for a transplant, *Biochem Biophys Res Commun*, 1992; 182(1):247–53.

23. Langsjoen, P. H., Langsjoen, P., Folkers, K., Isolated diagnostic dysfunction of the myocardium and its response to CoQ10 treatment, *Clin Invest*, 1993; 71(8):S140–4.

24. Langsjoen, P. H., et al., Usefulness of Coenzyme Q10 in clinical cardiology: A long-term study, *Mol Aspects Med*, 1994; 15:S165–75.

25. Permanetter, B., et al., Ubiquinone (Coenzyme Q10) in the long-term treatment of idiopathic dilated cardiomyopathy, *Eur Heart J*, 1992; 11:1528–33.

26. Lucker, P. W., et al., Pharmacokinetics of coenzyme ubidecarenone in healthy volunteers. In: Folkers, K., Yamamura, Y., (eds.), *Biomedical and clinical aspects of coenzyme Q*. Amsterdam: Elsevier, North Holland Biomedical Press, 1984; 143–151.

27. Chopra, R., Goldman, R., Bhagavan, H. N., Sinatra, S., A new Coenzyme Q10 preparation with enhanced relative bioavailability, *Nutrition Science News*, 1997; 2(2):88.

28. Chopra, R., Goldman, R., Sinatra, S., Bhagavan, H. N., Relative bioavailability of Coenzyme Q10 formulations in human subjects, *Int J Vitamin Nutr*, p 65. 1998.

29. Langsjoen, P. H., Folkers, K., Lyson, K., Muratsu, K., et al., Effective and safe therapy with coenzyme Q10 for cardiomyopathy. *Klin-Wochenschr*. 1988; 66(13):583–590.

30. Ernster, L., Forsmark, P., Ubiquinol: An endogenous antioxidant in aerobic organisms, *Clin Investig*, 1993; 71:S62.

31. Rauchova, H., Drahota, A., Lenaz, G., Function of Coenzyme Q in the cell: Some biochemical and physiological properties, *Physiol Res*, 1995; 44:209–216.

32. Chemey, R. H., Levy, D. K., Kalman, J., et al., Free radical activity increases with NYHA, class in congestive heart failure, *Am J Cardiol*, 1997; Supplement 29:2–102A.

33. Ganguly, P. K., Antioxidant therapy in congestive heart failure: Is there any advantage? *J Int Med*, 1991; 229:205–208.

34. Cowie, M. R., Penston, H., Wood, D. A., et al., A population survey of the incidence and aetiology of heart failure, *Am J Cardiol*, 1997; Supplement 29:30A.

35. Proceedings from American College of Cardiology: Women and Heart Disease. March 15, 1997.
36. Soja, A. M., Mortensen, S. A., Treatment of congestive heart failure with Coenzyme Q10 illuminated by meta-analyses of clinical trials, *Molecular Aspects of Medicine*, 1997; 18:S159–S168.
37. Sinatra, S. T., Refractory congestive heart failure successfully managed with high dose Coenzyme Q10 administration, *Molecular Aspects of Medicine*, 1997; 18:S299–S305.
38. Kim, Y., et al., Therapeutic effect of Coenzyme Q10 on idiopathic dilated cardiomyopathy: Assessment by iodine-123 labelled 15-(p-iodophenyl)-3(R,S)-methylpentadecanoic acid myocardial single-photon emission tomography, *European Journal of Nuclear Medicine*, 1997; 24:629–634.
39. Langsjoen, P., Langsjoen, A., Willis, R., Folkers, K., Treatment of hypertrophic cardiomyopathy with Coenzyme Q10. *Molecular Aspects of Med.* 1997; 18:S145–S151.

Chapter 6: Other Cardiovascular Applications: Hypertension, Angina, Mitral Valve Prolapse, Arrythmia, Atherosclerosis

1. Igarashi, T., Tanake, Y., Nakajima, Y., et al., Effect of Coenzyme Q10 on experimental hypertension in the desoxycorticosterone acetate-saline loaded rats, *Folic Pharm Jap*, 1972; 68:460.
2. Yamagami, T., Shibata, N., Folkers, K., Study of Coenzyme Q10 in essential hypertension. In: Folkers, K., Yamamura, Y., (eds.), Biomedical and Clinical Aspects of Coenzyme Q10, vol. 1, Amsterdam: Elsevier, 1977; 231–242.
3. Yamagami, T., Takagi, M., Akagami, H., Kubo, H., et al., Effect of Coenzyme Q10 on essential hypertension: a double-blind controlled study. In: Folkers, K., Yamamura, Y., (eds.), Biomedical and Clinical Aspects of Coenzyme Q10. vol 5, Elsevier Sci Publ B. V., Amsterdam, 1986; 337–343.
4. Digiesi, V., Cantini, F., Brodbeck, B., Effect of Coenzyme Q10 on essential arterial hypertension, *Curr Ther Res*, 1990; 5:841–845.
5. Langsjoen, P., Willis, R., Folkers, K., Treatment of essential hypertension with Coenzyme Q10, *Mol Aspects Med*, 1994; 15 (suppl):265–272.
6. Kamikawa, T., et al., Effects of Coenzyme Q10 on exercise tolerance in chronic stable angina pectoris, *Am J Cardiol*, 1985; 56:247–251.
7. Wilson, M. R., Frishman, W. H., Giles, T., et al., Coenzyme Q10 therapy and exercise duration in stable angina. In: Folkers, K., Littami, G. P., Yamogami, T., (eds.), Biomedical and Clinical Aspects of Coenzyme Q, vol. 6, Amsterdam: Elsevier; 1991: 339–348.

8. Schardt, F., et al., Effect of Coenzyme Q10 on ischemia-induced ST-segment depression: A double-blind placebo-controlled crossover study. In: Folkers, K., Yamamura, Y., (eds.), Biomedical and Clinical Aspects of Coenzyme Q10, vol 5, Amsterdam, Elsevier, 1986; 385–394.

9. Oda, T., Coenzyme Q10 therapy on the cardiac dysfunction in patients with mitral valve prolapse. Dose vs. effect and dose vs. serum level of Coenzyme Q10. In: Folkers, K., Yamamura, Y., (eds.), Biomedical and Clinical Aspects of Coenzyme Q10, vol 5, Elsevier Sci Publ B. V., Amsterdam, 1986; 269–289.

10. Nogai, S., Migazuki, Y., Ogawa, K., Satake, T., et al., The effect of Coenzyme Q10 on reperfusion injury in canine myocardium, *J Mol Cell Cardiol*, 1985; 17:873–878.

11. Husono, K., Ishida, H., et al., Protective effects of Coenzyme Q10 against arrhythmia and its intracellular distribution. A study on the cultured single myocardial cell. In: Folkers, K., Yamamura, Y., (eds.): Biomedical and Clinical Aspects of Coenzyme Q10, vol 3, Elsevier/North Holland Biomedical Press, Amsterdam, 1981: 269–278.

12. Otani, T., Tanaka, H., Onoue, T., et al., In vitro study on contribution of oxidative metabolism of isolated rabbit heart mitochondria to myocardial reperfusion injury, *Circ Res*, 1984; 55:168–175.

13. Fujioka, T., Sakamoto, Y., Mimura, G., Clinical study of cardiac arrhythmias using a 24-hour continuous electrocardiographic recorder (5th report) — Antiarrhythmic action of Coenzyme Q10 in diabetes, *Tohoku J Exp Med*, 1983; 141(Suppl):453–463.

14. Ohnishi, S., et al., The effect of Coenzyme Q10 on premature ventricular contraction. In: Folkers, K., Yamamura, Y., (eds.), Biomedical and Clinical Aspects of Coenzyme Q10, vol 5. Elsevier Sci. Publ. B. V., Amsterdam, 1986: 257–266.

15. Kuklinski, B., Weissenbacher, E., Fahnrich, A., Coenzyme Q10 and antioxidants in acute myocardial infarction. *Mol Aspects Med*, 1994; 15(suppl):S143–S147.

16. Singh, R. B., et al., Usefulness of antioxidant vitamins in suspected acute myocardial infarction (the Indian experiment of infarct survival-3). *Am J of Cardiol*, 1996; 77:232–236.

17. Chen, Y. F., Lin, Y. T., Wu, S. C., Effectiveness of Coenzyme Q10 on myocardial preservation during hypotherimic cardioplegic arrest, *J thorac Cardiovas Surg*, 1994; 107:242–7.

18. Sunamori, M., Tanaka, H., Marvyama, T., et al., Clinical experience of CoQ10 to enhance interoperative myocardial protection in coronary artery revascularization, *Cardiovasc Drug Therapy*, 1991; 5 Suppl 2:297–300.

19. Tanaka, J., Tominaga, R., Yoshitoshi, M., et al., Coenzyme Q10: The pro-

phylactic effect of low cardiac output following cardiac valve replacement, *Ann Thorac Surg*, 1982; 33:145–51.

20. Naylar, W. G., The use of Coenzyme Q10 to ischaemia heart muscle. In: Yamamura, Y., Folkers, K., Ito, Y., (eds.): Biomedical and Clinical Aspects of Coenzyme Q, vol 2; Elsevier, North Holland, Biomedical Press, Amsterdam, 1980: 409–425.

21. Coghlan, J. G., Madden, B., Norell, M. N., et al., Lipid peroxidation and changes in vitamin E levels during coronary artery bypass grafting. *J Thorac Cardiovas Surg*. 1993; 106:268–74.

22. Mehta, J., Yang, G., Nichols, W., Free radicals, antioxidants and coronary heart disease, *J Myocardial Ischemia*, 1993; 5:31–41.

23. Greenberg, S. M., Frishman, W. H., Coenzyme Q10: A new drug for cardiovascular disease, *J Clin Pharmacol*, 1990; 30:596–608.

24. Shlafer, M., Kane, D. F., Kirsh, M. M., Superoxide dismutase plus catalase enhance the efficacy of hypothermic cardioplegia to protect the globally ischemic, reperfused heart. *J Thorac Cardiovasc Surg*, 1982; 83:8:30–9.

25. Myers, M. I., Bolli, R., Lekich, R., et al., Enhancement of recovery of myocardial function by oxygen free radical scavengers after reversible regional ischemia, *Circulation*, 1985; 72:915–21.

26. Ohhara, H., Kanaide, H., Yoshimura, R., et al., Protective effect of coenzyme Q10 on ischaemia and reperfusion of the isolated perfused rat heart, *J Mol Cell Cardiol*, 1981; 13:65.

27. Belch, J. J. F., Free radicals and their scavenging in stroke, *Scottish Med* 1992; 37:67–8.

28. Steinberg, D., Pathasarathy, S., Carew, T. E., et al., Beyond cholesterol: Modifications of low-density lipoprotein that increase its atherogenicity, *N Engl J Med*, 1989; 320:915–24.

29. Mohr, D., Bowry, W. W., Stocker, R., Dietary supplementation with Coenzyme Q10 results in increased levels of ubiquinol-10 within circulating lipidprotein and increased resistance of human low-density lipoprotein to the initiation of lipid peroxidation, *Biochim Biophys Acta*, 1992; 1126:247–254.

30. Galle, J., Mulsch, A., Busse, R., Bassenge, E., Effects of native and oxidized low-density lipoproteins on formation and inactivation of endothelium-derived relaxing factor, *Arterioscler Thromb*, 1991; 11:198–203.

31. Esterbauer, H., Dieber-Rotheneder, M., Striegl, G., et al., Role of vitamin E in preventing oxidation of low-density lipoprotein, *Am J Clin Nutr*, 1991; 53:314S–21S.

32. Parthasarathy, S., Rankin, S. M., Role of oxidized low-density lipoprotein in atherogenesis, *Prog Lipid Res*, 1991; 31:127–43.

33. Sinatra, S. T., DeMarco, J., Free radicals, oxidative stress, oxidized low-

density lipoprotein (LDL), and the heart: Antioxidants and other strategies to limit cardiovascular damage, *CT Medicine*, 1995; 59:579–588.

34. Jialal, I., Fuller, C. J., Oxidized LDL and antioxidants, *Clin Cardiol*, 1993; 16 (Suppl I):I–6–I–9.

35. Palinkski, W., Rosenfeld, M. E., Yla-Herttuala, S., et al., Low-density lipoprotein undergoes oxidative modification in vivo, *Proc Natl Acad Sci, USA*, 1989; 86:1372–6.

36. Morel, D. W., Hessler, J. R., Chisolm, G. M., Low-density lipoprotein cytotoxicity induced by free radical peroxidation of lipid, *J Lipid Res*, 1983; 24:1070–6.

37. Esterbauer, H., et al., Continuous monitoring of in vitro oxidation of human low-density lipoproteins, *Free Rad Res Commun*, 1989; 6:67–75.

38. Reaven, P., Khouw, A., Belz, W., et al., Effect of dietary antioxidant combinations in humans, *Arterioscler Thromb*, 1993; 13:590–600.

39. Frei, B., Kim, M. C., Ames, B. N., Ubiquinol-10 is an effective lipid-soluble antioxidant at physiological concentrations, *Proc Natl Acad Sci, USA* 1990; 87:48–79–4883.

40. Bowry, V. W., et al., Prevention of tocopherol-mediated peroxidation in ubiquinol-10-free human low-density lipoprotein, *J Biol Chem*, 1995; 270(11):5756–63.

41. Ingold, K. U., et al., Autoxidation of lipids and antioxidation by alpha-tocopherol and ubiquinol in homogeneous solution and in aqueous dispersions of lipids: unrecognized consequences of lipid particle size as exemplified by oxidation of human low-density lipoprotein, *Proc Natl Acad Sci, USA*, 1993; 90(1):45–49.

42. Thomas, S. R., Neuzil, J., Stocker, R., Inhibition of LDL oxidation by Ubiquinol-10. A protective Mechanism for Coenzyme Q in atherogenesis? In: Littarru, G. P., Alleva, R., Battino, M., Folkers, K., (eds.) *Mol Aspects of Med*, 1997; Suppl 18:S1–S309.

Chapter 7: Thyroid, Adriamycin and Coenzyme Q10

1. Suzuki, H., et al., Cardiac performance and Coenzyme Q10 in thyroid disorders, *Endocrinol Japan*, 1984; 31:755.

2. Kishi, Y., et al., Protective effect of Coenzyme Q on Adriamycin toxicity in beating heart cells, In: *Biomedical and Clinical Aspects of Coenzyme Q*, vol. 4, Folkers, K., Yamamura, Y., (eds.). Elsevier, 1984:181–188.

3. Ogura, R., et al., The role of ubiquinone (Coenzyme Q10) in preventing Adriamycin-induced mitochondrial disorders in rat heart, *J Appl Biochem*, 1979; 1:325–335.

4. Karlsson, J., et al., Effect of Adriamycin on heart and skeletal muscle Coen-

zyme Q (CoQ10) in man. In: Folkers, K. and Yamamura, Y., (eds.). *Biomedical and Clinical Aspects of Coenzyme Q*. vol. 5, Elsevier, 1986.

5. Judy, W. V., et al., Coenzyme Q10 reduction of Adriamycin cardiotoxicity. In Folkers, K., Yamamura, Y. (eds.). *Biomedical and Clinical Aspects of Coenzyme Q*, vol. 4, Elsevier, 1984:231–241.

6. Faure, H., et al., 5-hydroxymethyluracil excretion, plasma TBARS and plasma antioxidant vitamins in Adriamycin-treated patients, *Free Rad Biol Med*, 1996; 20:979–983.

7. Iarussi, D., et al., Protective effect of Coenzyme Q on anthracyclines cardiotoxicity; control study in children with acute lymphoblastic leukemia or non-Hodgkin limphoma, *Molecular Aspects of Medicine*, 1994.

8. Henderson, C., et al., Serial studies of cardiac function in patients receiving Adriamycin, *Cancer Treat, Rep*, 1978; 63:923.

9. Cortes, E. P., et al., Adriamycin cardiotoxicity: Early detection by systolic time interval and possible prevention by Coenzyme Q10, *Cancer Treat Rep*, 1978; 62:887–891.

Chapter 8: Optimum Aging

1. Harman, D., Aging: A theory based on free radical and radiation chemistry, *J Gerontol*, 1956; 11:298–300.

2. Beyer, R. E., Ernster, L., The antioxidant role of Coenzyme Q. In: Lenaz, G., et al., (eds.): *Highlights in Ubiquinone Research*. Taylor and Francis, London, 1990: 191–213.

3. Kalen, A., Appelkvist, E. L., Dallner, G., Age-related changes in the lipid composition of rat and human tissue, *Lipids*, 1989; 24:579–584.

4. Baumgartner, R. N., Body composition in elderly persons: a critical review of needs and methods, *Prog Food Nutr Sci*, 1993; 17:223–260.

5. Vaughan, L., Zurlo F., Ravussin, E., Aging and energy expenditure, *Am J Clin Nurs*, 1991; 53:821–825.

6. Linnane, A. W., The Universality of Bioenergetic Disease an Amelioration Therapy: Coenzyme Q10 and Analogues. Proceedings of: The 9th International Symposium on Biomedical and Clinical Aspects of Coenzyme Q, 1996.

7. Villalba, J. M., et al. Role of cytochrome b_5 reductase on the antioxidant function of Coenzyme Q in the plasma membrane, *Molec Aspects Med*, 1997; 8(suppl) s7–s13.

8. Ravaglia, G., Forti, P., Maioli, F., et al., Coenzyme Q10 plasma levels and body composition in elderly males, *Arch Gerontal Geriatr* 1996; 5:539–543.

9. Soderberg, M., Lipid composition of different regions of the human brain during aging, *J Neurochem*, 1990; 54(2):415–423.

Chapter 9: Immunity and Defense

1. Mayer, P., Hamberger, H., Drews, J., Differential effects of ubiquinone Q7 and ubiquinone analogs on macrophage activation and experimental infections in granulocytopenic mice, *Infection*, 1980; 8:256–261.
2. Saiki, I., Tokushima, Y., Nishimura, K., Azuma, I., Macrophage activation with ubiquinone and their related compounds in mice, *Int J Vitam Nutr Res*, 1983; 53:312–320.
3. Bliznakov, E., Casey, A., Premuzic, E., Coenzyme Q: stimulants of the phagocytic activity in rats and immune response in mice, *Experientia*, 1970; 26:953–954.
4. Coles, L. S., Harris, S. B., Coenzyme Q10 and Lifespan Extension. In: *Advances in Antiaging Medicine*. Ed: Klatz, R. M., Mary Ann Liebert, Inc. Pub. New York, N.Y., 1996; 205–215.
5. Folkers, K., Shizukuishi, S., Takemura, K., et al., Increase in levels of IgG in serum of patients treated with Coenzyme Q10, *Res Commun Chem Pathol Pharmacol*, 1982; 38:335–338.
6. Folkers, K., Langsjoen, P., Nara, Y., et al., Biochemical deficiencies of Coenzyme Q10 in HIV-infection and exploratory treatment, *Biochem Biophys Res Commun*, 1988; 153:888–896.
7. Langsjoen, P., Folkers, K., Richardson, P., Treatment of patients with human immunodeficiency virus infection with Coenzyme Q10. *Elsevier Science Publishers* 1991; 409–415.

Chapter 10: Cancer: Public Enemy #1

1. Bliznakov, E. G., Effect of stimulation of the host defense system by Coenzyme Q10 on dibenzpyrene-induced tumors and infection with Friend leukemia virus in mice, *Proc Natl Acad Sci*, 1973; 70:390–394.
2. Atroshi, F., Rizzo, A., Biese, I., et al., T-2 Toxin-induced DNA Damage in Mouse Livers: the Effect of Pretreatment with Coenzyme Q10 and *a*-Tocopherol. In: *Molecular Aspects of Medicine*. Littarru, G. P., Alleva, R., Battino, M., Folkers, K. (eds.). 1997; suppl. 18:S255–58.
3. Lockwood, K., et al., Progress on therapy of breast cancer with vitamin Q10 and the regression of metastases, *Biochem Biophys Res Commun*, 1995; 212(1):
4. Waters, D., Higginson, L., Gladstone, P., et al., Effects of monotherapy with an HMG-CoA reductase inhibitors on the progression of coronary atherosclerosis as assessed by serial quantitative arteriography: the Canadian Coronary Atherosclerosis Intervention Trial, *Circulation*, 1994; 89:959–968.
5. Folkers, K., Relevance of the biosynthesis of Coenzyme Q10 and of the

four bases of DNA as a rationale for the molecular causes of cancer and a therapy, *Biochem Biophys Res Commun,* 1996; 224(2):358–61.

6. Folkers, K., et al., Unpublished manuscript.
7. Folkers, K., et al., Activities of Vitamin Q10 in animal models and a serious deficiency in patients with cancer, *Biochem Biophys Res Commun,* 1997; 234(2):296–9.
8. Hanioka, T., et al., *J of Dental Health,* 1993; 43(5):667–672.
9. Folkers, K., Ellis, J., Yang, O., et al., *Vitamins and Cancer Prevention.* 1991; 8:103–110.
10. Personal communications with Dr. Kenneth Cooper.

Chapter 11: Periodontal Disease

1. Littarru, G. P., et al., Deficiency of Coenzyme Q10 in gingival tissue from patients with periodontal disease, *Proc Natl Acad Sci,* 1971; 68:2332–2335.
2. Hanioka, T., et al., Therapy with Coenzyme Q10 for patients with periodontal disease. Effect of Coenzyme Q10 on the immune system, *J of Dental Health,* 1993; 43:667–672.
3. McRee, J. T., et al., Therapy with Coenzyme Q10 for patients with periodontal disease. Effect of Coenzyme Q10 on subgingival microorganisms, *J of Dental Health,* 1993; 43:659–666.
4. Shizukuishi, S., et al., Clinical effect of Coenzyme Q10 on periodontal disease: Evaluation of oxygen utilization in gingiva by tissue reflectance spectrophotometry. In: *Biomedical and clinical aspects of Coenzyme Q10.* Editors: Folkers, K., Yamamura, Y., Elsevier, Amsterdam, 1986; 5:359–368.
5. Iwamoto, Y., et al., Clinical effects of Coenzyme Q10 on periodontal disease. *Biomedical and clinical aspects of Coenzyme Q10,* 1981; 3:109–119.
6. Wilkinson, E. G., Arnold, R. M., Folkers, K., Treatment of periodontal and other soft-tissue diseases of the oral cavity with Coenzyme Q. In Folkers, K., Yamamura, Y., (eds.). *Biomedical and Clinical Aspects of Coenzyme Q10,* vol. 1, Elsevier/North-Holland Biomedical Press, Amsterdam, 1977; pp. 251–265.
7. Bliznakov, E. G., Hunt, G. L., *The Miracle Nutrient—Coenzyme Q10.* New York: Bantam, 1987.
8. Watts, T. L. P., Coenzyme Q10 and periodontal treatment: Is there any beneficial effect? *Br Dent J,* 1995; 178:209–213.

Chapter 12: Neurodegenerative Diseases

1. Beal, M. F., Does impairment of energy metabolism result in excitotoxic neuronal death in neurodegenerative illnesses? *Annals of Neurology,* 1992; 31:119–130.

2. Beal, M. F., Aging, energy and oxidative stress in neurodegenerative diseases, *Annals of Neurology*, 1995; 38:357–366.

3. Beal, M. F., et al., Coenzyme Q10 and nicotinamide block striatal lesions produced by the mitochondrial toxin malonate, *Annals of Neurology*, 1994; 36:882–888.

4. Beal, M. F. and Matthews, R. T., Coenzyme Q10 in the central nervous system and its potential usefulness in the treatment of neurodegenerative diseases, *Molec Aspects Med*, 1997; 18:169–179.

5. Koroshetz, W. J., et al., Assessment of energy metabolism defects in Huntington's disease and possible therapy with Coenzyme Q10, *Annals of Neurology*, 1997; 41:160–165.

6. Imagawa, M., et al., Coenzyme Q10, iron, and vitamin B_6 in genetically confirmed Alzheimer's disease, *The Lancet*, 1992; 340:671.

7. Sano, M., et al., A controlled trial of selegiline, alpha-tocopherol or both as treatment for Alzheimer's disease, *N Eng J of Med*, 1997; 336:1216–22.

8. Edlund, C., Soderberg, M., Kristensson, K., Isoprenoids in aging and neurodegeneration, *Neurochemistry Intl*, 1994; 25:35–38.

9. Shults, C. W., et al., Coenzyme Q10 levels correlate with the activities of complexes I and II/III in mitochondria from Parkinsonian and non-Parkinsonian subjects, *Annals of Neurology*, 1997; 42:261–264.

10. Fariello, R. G., et al., Regional distribution of ubiquinones and tocopherols in the mouse brain: lowest content of ubiquinols in the *substantia nigra*, *Neuropharmacology*, 1988; 27:1077–1080.

11. Strijks, E., Kremer, H. P. H., Horstink, M. W. I. M., Q10 therapy in patients with idiopathic Parkinson's disease, *Mol Aspects Med*, 1997; 18:237–240.

12. Tipton K. F., Singer T. P.: Advances in our understanding of the mechanisms of the neurotoxicity of MPTP and related compounds. *J of Neurochemistry*, 1993; 61:1191–1206.

13. Fallon, J., et al., MPP + produces progressive neuronal degeneration which is mediated by oxidative stress, *Exp Neurol*, 1997; 144(1):193 – 8.

14. Birkmayer, G. D., *NADH:The Energizing CoEnzyme*. Keats Publishing, Inc., New Canaan, CT 1997.

15. Linnane A. W., et al., Mitochondrial DNA mutation and the aging process: bioenergy and pharmacological intervention, *Mutation Research*, 1992; 275:195–208.

Chapter 13: Diabetes

1. Salonen, J. T., Nyyssonen, K., Tuomainen, T. P., et al., Increased risk of noninsulin-dependent diabetes mellitus at low plasma vitamin E concen-

trations: A four-year follow-up study in men, Research Institute of Public Health, University of Kuopio, Finland, *BMJ*, 1995, 28;311:1124–7.

2. Esterbauer, H., Rotheneder, M., Striegl, G. Vitamin E and other lipophilic antioxidants protect LDL against oxidation. *Fat Sci Technol* 1989; 91:316–324.

3. Kishi, T., et al., Bioenergetics in clinical medicine, studies on Coenzyme Q and diabetes mellitus, *J Medicine*, 1976; 7:307.

4. Jameson, S., Statistical data support prediction of death within six months on low levels of Coenzyme Q10 and other entities, *Clin Investig*, 1993; 71:S137–S139.

5. McDonnell, M. G., Archbold, G. P. R., Plasma ubiquinol/cholesterol ratios in patients with hyperlipaemia, those with diabetes mellitus and in patients requiring dialysis. *Clinica Chimica Acta*, 1996; 117–126.

6. Shigeta, Y., Izumik, A. H., Effect of Coenzyme Q7 treatment on blood sugars and ketone bodies of diabetics, *J Vitaminol*, 1966; 12:293; 1966.

7. Andersen, C. B., Henriksen, J. E., Hother-Nielsen, O. H., et al., The effect of Coenzyme Q10 on blood glucose and insulin requirement in patients with insulin-dependent diabetes mellitus, *Molec Aspects Med*, 1997; 18:s307–s309.

8. Singh, R. B., et al., Effect of Coenzyme Q10 on Plasma Insulin Levels and Oxidative Stress in Patients with Acute Myocardial Infarction, 1998; Submitted for publication.

Chapter 14: Other Pathogenic Conditions: Chronic Obstructive Pulmonary Disease, Obesity, Skin Damage

1. Fujimoto, S., et al., Effects of Coenzyme Q10 administration on pulmonary function and exercise performance in patients with chronic lung disease, *Clin Investig*, 1993; 71(8 Suppl):S162–6.

2. Karlsson, J., Diamant, B., Folkers, K., Exercise-limiting factors in respiratory distress. *Respiration*, 1992; 59 Suppl 2:18–23.

3. Selivanof, V., et al., Nutrition's role in averting respiratory failure. *J Respiratory Dis*, 1983; 4(9),29.

4. Van Gaal, L., et al., Exploratory study of Coenzyme Q10 and obesity. In: Folkers, K., Yamamara, Y., (eds.) *Biomed and Clin Aspects of CoQ10*, vol. 4, Elsevier Publ. 1984; pp. 369–373.

5. Poda, M., Packer, L., Ubiquinol, a marker of oxidative stress in skin. Proceedings at the 9th International Symposium on Biomedical and Clinical Aspects of CoQ10, Ancona, Italy, 1996.

6. Hoppe, U., et al., Coenzyme Q10—a Cutaneous Antioxidant and Energizer. Presented at the First Conference of the International Coenzyme Q10 Association, 1998.

Chapter 15: New Hope for Male Infertility

1. Stansbury, J., Fortifying fertility with vitamins and herbs, *Nutr Sci News*, 1997; 12(2):606–612.
2. Oeda, T., Henkel, R., Ohmori, H., et al., Scavenging effect of N-Acetyl-L-Cysteine against reactive oxygen species in human semen: A possible therapeutic modality for male factor infertility? *J Andrology*, 1997; 29:125–131.
3. Lewin, A., et al., The Effect of Coenzyme Q10 on Sperm Motility and Function. *Mole Aspects Med*, 1997; 18(suppl):s213–s219.
4. Angelitti, A. G., Colacicco, L., Calla, C., et al., Coenzyme Q: Potentially useful index of bioenergetic and oxidative status of spermatozoa, *Clin Chem*, 1995; 41:217–219.
5. Jones, R., Mann, T., Damage to ram spermatozoa by peroxidation of endogenous phospholipids, *Journal of Reproduction and Fertility*, 1977; 50:261–268.
6. Beyer, R. E., Ernster, L., The antioxidant role of Coenzyme Q. In *Highlights in Ubiquinone Research*, Lenaz, G., Barnabei, O., et al., (eds.) Taylor and Francis, London. 1990; 191–213.
7. Mazzilli, F., Bisanti, A., Rossi, T., et al., Seminal and biological parameters in dyspermic patients with sperm hypomotility before and after treatment with Ubiquinone, *Journal of Endocrinological Investigations*, 1990; 13(suppl 1):88.
8. Aitken, R. J., Clarkson, J. S., Significance of reactive oxygen species and antioxidants in defining the efficacy of sperm preparation techniques, *Journal of Andrology*, 1988; 9:367–376.
9. Geva, E., Bartoov, B., Zabludovsky, N., et al., The effect of antioxidant treatment on human spermatozoa and fertilization rate in an in vitro fertilization program. *Annual Meeting of the Israeli Fertility Association*, 1996 (May 6–7) p. 47.
10. Alleva R., et al., The protective role of Ubiquinol-10 against formation of lipid hydroperoxides in human seminal fluid, *Mole Aspects Med*, 1997; 18(suppl):s221–s228.

Chapter 16: Coenzyme Q10 and the Athlete

1. Walker, B. F., Roberts, W. C., Sudden death while running in conditioned runners aged 40 years or over, *Am J Cardiol*, 1980; 45(6):1292.
2. Karlsson, et al., Plasma, ubiquinone, Alpha tocopherol and cholesterol in man, *International J Vit Nutr Research*, 1992; 62(2):160–4.
3. Battino, M., et al., Metabolic and antioxidant markers in the plasma of

sportsmen from a Mediterranean town performing non-agonistic activity, *Molec Aspects Med*, 1997; Vol. 18 (Supplement), pp. s241–s245.

4. Littarru, G. P., Energy and Defense, Casa Editrice Scientifica Internazionale, Rome. 1995.
5. Shimomura, Y., et al., Protective effect of Coenzyme Q10 on exercise-induced muscular injury, *Biochem Biophy Res Comm* 1991, 176:349–55.
6. Fiorella, P. L., et al., Metabolic effects of Coenzyme Q10 treatment in high-level athletes. In: *Biomedical and Clinical Aspects of Coenzyme Q*, 1991, Vol. 6. Folkers, K., Yamagami, T., Littarru, G. P., (eds.) Elsevier, pp. 613–520.
7. Vanfaechem, J. H. P. and Folkers, K., Coenzyme Q10 and physical performance. In: *Biomedical and Clinical Aspects of Coenzyme Q*, 1981; vol 3. Folkers, K. and Yamamura, Y. (eds.) Elsevier/North-Holland Biomedical Press, Amsterdam, 1981, pp. 235–241.
8. Ylikoski, T., et al., The effect of Coenzyme Q10 on the exercise performance of cross-country skiers, *Molec Aspects Med*, 1997, Vol. 18 (Supplement), pp. S283–s290, 1997.
9. Weston, S. B., et al., Does exogenous coenzyme Q10 affect aerobic capacity in endurance athletes? *Int J Sport Nutr* 1997 Sep;7(3):197–206.
10. Porter, D. A., et al., The effect of oral Coenzyme Q10 on the exercise tolerance of middle-aged, untrained men, *Int J Sports Med*, 1995, 16(7):421–7.
11. Snider, I. P., et al., Effects of coenzyme athletic performance system as an ergogenic aid on endurance performance to exhaustion, *Int J Sport Nutr* 1992; 2(3):272–86.

Chapter 17: Muscular Dystrophy and Mitochondrial Encephalopathy

1. Folkers, K., Wolianuk, J., et al., Biochemical rationale and the cardiac response of patients with muscle disease to therapy with Coenzyme Q10, *Proc Natl Acad Sci*, 1985; 82:4513–4516.
2. Folkers, K., Simonsen, R., Two successful double-blind trials with Coenzyme Q10 (vitamin Q10) and muscular dystrophies and neurogenic atrophies, Source: *Biochim Biophys Acta*, 1995; 1271(1):281–6.
3. Bendahan, D., et al., PNMR spectroscopy and ergometer exercise test as evidence for muscle oxidative performance improvement with Coenzyme Q in mitochondrial myopathies, *Neurology*, 1992; 42:1203–1208.
4. Barbiroli, B., et al., Coenzyme Q10 improves mitochondrial respiration in patients with mitochondrial cytopathies. An in vivo study on brain and skeletal muscle by phosphorus magnetic resonance spectroscopy, *Cell Mol Biol*, 1997; 43(5):741–9.

5. Seki, A., et al., Mitochondrial encephalomyopathy with 15915 mutation: Clinical report, *Pediatr Neurol*, 1997; 17(2):161–4.
6. Chariot, P., et al., Simvastatin-induced rhabdomyolysis followed by a MELAS syndrome, *Amer J of Med*, 1993; 94:109.

Chapter 18: Side Effects, Contraindications, Drug Interactions

1. Greenberg, S., and Frishman, W. H., Coenzyme Q10: A new drug for cardiovascular disease, *Clin Pharm*, 1990; 30:596–608.
2. Feigin, A., et al., Assessment of Coenzyme Q10 tolerability in Huntington's disease, *Mov Disord*, 1996; 11(3):321–3.
3. Noia, G., et al., Coenzyme Q10 in pregnancy, *Fetal Diagn Ther*, 1996; 11(4):264–70.
4. Noia, G., et al., Blood levels of Coenzyme Q10 in early phase of normal or complicated pregnancies. In: *Biomedical and Clinical Aspects of Coenzyme Q*, Folkers, K., Yamamura, Y. (eds.), Amsterdam, Esevier, 1991; 6:209–213.
5. Kishi, T., Kishi, H., and Folkers, K., Inhibition of cardiac CoQ10-enzymes by clinically used drugs and possible prevention, In: *Biomedical and Clinical Aspects of Coenzyme Q*, Vol 1. Folkers, K. and Yamamura, Y. (eds.). Elsevier/North-Holland Biomedical Press, Amsterdam, 1977, pp. 47–62.
6. Hamada, M., Kazatani, Y., Ochi, T., et al., Correlation between serum CoQ10 level and myocardial contractility in hypertensive patients. In: *Biomedical and Clinical Aspects of Coenzyme Q*, Vol 4. Folkers, K. and Yamamura, Y. (eds.). Elsevier Science Publ, Amsterdam, 1984, pp. 263–270.
7. Kishi, T., Makino, K., Okamoto, T., et al., Inhibition of myocardial respiration by psychotherapeutic drugs and prevention by Coenzyme Q. In: *Biomedical and Clinical Aspects of Coenzyme Q*, Vol 2. Yamamura, Y., Folkers, K., and Ito, Y. (eds.). Elsevier/North-Holland Biomedical Press, Amsterdam, 1980, pp. 139–154.
8. Ibid.
9. Spigset, O., Reduced effect of warfarin caused by ubidecarenone. In: *The Lancet*, Vol 344; 1994:1372–1373.

Chapter 19: Conclusion: The Future of CoQ10

1. Christensen, J., et al., Fish consumption, n-3 fatty acids in cell membranes and heart rate variability in survivors of myocardial infarction with left ventricular dysfunction. *Am J Cardiol.*, 1997; 79:1670–1673.7.
2. De Lorgeril, M., et al., Effect of a Mediterranean type of diet on the rate of cardiovascular complications in patients with coronary artery disease. *J Am Coll Cardiol.*, 1996; 28:1103–1108.

3. De Lorgeril, M., et al., What makes a Mediterranean diet, cardio- protective? *Cardio Rev.*, 1997; 14:15–21.

4. Siscovick, D., et al., Dietary intake and cell membrane levels of long-chain n-3 polyunsaturated fatty acids and the risk of primary cardiac arrest. *JAMA* 1995; 274:1363–1367.

Index